THERE'S POWER IN THE CONNECTION

BUILDING A NETWORK OF DYNAMIC CONGREGATIONS

LARRY M. GOODPASTER

Abingdon Press
Nashville

THERE'S POWER IN THE CONNECTION
BUILDING A NETWORK OF DYNAMIC CONGREGATIONS

Library of Congress Cataloging-in-Publication Data

Goodpaster, Larry M., 1948-
    There's power in the connection : building a network of dynamic congregations / Larry M. Goodpaster.
        p. cm.
    ISBN 978-0-687-64979-2 (binding: pbk., adhesive-perfect : alk. paper)
    1. Church growth. 2. Church renewal. 3. Evangelistic work. 4. United Methodist Church (U.S.). Alabama-West Florida Conference. I. Title.
    BV652.25.G66 2008
    254'.076--dc22

                                                                        2007037054

08 09 10 11 12 13 14 15 16 17—10 9 8 7 6 5 4 3 2 1
MANUFACTURED IN THE UNITED STATES OF AMERICA

To the people of the Alabama–West Florida Conference

of The United Methodist Church

The surviving remnant of the house of Judah shall

again take root downward, and bear fruit upward.

—*2 Kings 19:30*

CONTENTS

PREFACE

Like many families, ours has developed a number of rituals surrounding the Christmas season. One of those is simply that we enjoy the old classic Christmas movies like *Miracle on Thirty-Fourth Street*, *It's a Wonderful Life*, and *Holiday Inn* (black-and-white versions, please). In one of our favorites, *Christmas in Connecticut*, Barbara Stanwyck portrays a magazine columnist who writes a regular feature on cooking. Unfortunately, she cannot cook, and most of her copy is pure fiction, which, with the help and support of a few friends, including Felix (the real chef), grows out of her very creative imagination. Over a Christmas holiday, however, her secret is discovered by her publisher-boss. Near the end of the film she launches into a tirade with him. We have seen the movie so many times that we can recite the words along with her: "Suppose you listen to me. I'm tired of being pushed around, tired of being told what to do, tired of writing your gall darn articles, tired of dancing to everybody else's tune, tired of being told whom to marry. In short—I'm tired."

Frankly I am tired! I am weary of being told that The United Methodist Church is on its last leg; that the decline of membership signals the demise of the denomination; that Christendom is dead; that the only churches that can possibly grow in the current environment are those that are rigidly right politically and socially, and, in a word, fundamentalist; and that those of us in leadership positions are like leaders on the *Titanic*: the blow is struck, the ship is sinking, the chairs are being shuffled, and the end is near. Likewise, from the other side, I am weary of being told that all is well; that if we just work a little harder with what we have, everything will be fine; that if one group or the other will just leave, "we" (whoever that is) will survive; that evangelism is an outdated, irrelevant word and that even speaking of it turns people off; and that the larger the bureaucracy grows and the deeper ingrained the institution becomes, the more solutions will be found.

Somewhere between these extremes there is hope! As a bishop in The United Methodist Church, I am confronted with the challenge of walking an ever-thinning line: holding the institution together, keeping it on track, but envisioning and leading toward a different day and a different church. John Wesley faced similar circumstances: declining church attendance; lagging enthusiasm and loyalty to Jesus; magnificent, but empty, structures; highly trained, well-educated, but ineffective priests; generations of people going through the motions of life without the life-renewing, life-empowering, life-transforming presence of Jesus Christ.

As 2007 dawned, I discovered a verse that has now become a daily companion. I have meditated upon it, contemplated it, studied it, and, in general, allowed it to take up residence in my life. Second Kings is a history book that includes miraculous moments, tragic moments, and holy moments. It records the names and exploits of the kings of the divided monarchy (Israel and Judah) and, often with the briefest of commentary, categorizes those leaders as either doing right or wrong in the sight of God while the countries thrive or crumble around them. The northern kingdom falls into the hands of the Assyrians, and the southern kingdom will not be far behind. It was there, in the midst of that sequence of events, that I stumbled upon this verse that now I ponder anew in the context of The United Methodist Church; 2 Kings 19:30 reads, "The surviving remnant of the house of Judah shall again take root downward, and bear fruit upward."

This book is about putting down roots—again. It is about recovering something of who we have been and what we might yet be. While serving as a pastor in Mississippi for three decades (parts of four if my years as a student pastor are added), I watched The United Methodist Church record annual declines. For all of my ordained life, the denomination that nurtured me, credentialed me, and sent me to places of service has been in a free fall, and today we are either in denial or despair. The "we" is a collective and all-inclusive "we"—laypeople and clergy, bishops and denominational executives, members and constituents, female and male, young and old (although, regrettably, there is a decreasing number of the young to worry about all of this). "We" all want the denomination to bear fruit, to do good things in the world, to stand for justice and mercy, to offer hope and hospitality in this broken world. But, as the writer of 2 Kings reminded the remnant (those still hanging on and hanging around), if we want to bear fruit, we first start with the foundation, the root system, the core of who we are. Let it grow from the ground up. Our future is and must be about the grass roots and the shaping influence that must happen at the point where the gospel interacts with and invades the hearts and lives of individuals in local churches.

When I was assigned to the Alabama–West Florida Conference in 2000 following my election as a bishop in The United Methodist Church, I could not imagine what I was about to encounter, how different my life would be, or what I would come to learn and experience in this office in this place. This book grows out of that experience, and is intended to offer hope to a denomination that proclaims hope, but seems to have little for itself or its future. The thesis that will be unfolding in the following pages is about the root system of the church and about the hope that can transform us. In essence, this will be about an infusion of God's holy, gracious, and transforming power to and for the connection. Although the approach is distinctly United Methodist, the principles and guidelines are applicable across denominational lines. My conviction is that hope for the future of The United Methodist Church will be rediscovered through the interaction of three vital signs: clergy excellence, congregational health, and Wesleyan theology.

Excellent clergy leadership has been, and is now, a crucial element in the turnaround of this or any denomination. Effective pastoral leaders for the twenty-first century will exhibit qualities that combine both the skills that are taught and developed and grace-gifts that are received and nurtured. Effective pastoral-leaders will call forth and equip others to exercise their unique ministry and to live out of their passion for following Jesus. Partnerships will be created in order to fulfill God's mission in the world through the church. Becoming a healthy, dynamic, thriving congregation that responds to human need by loving God and neighbor and that offers hope, healing, and hospitality to a fragmented, disjointed, violent world is the urgent need for this twenty-first century. This is Wesley's vision of perfection, a call and challenge that those of us who stand in that tradition must reclaim. A recovery and renewal of Wesleyan theology for the twenty-first century lived out in healthy congregations led by excellent pastors is what is called for in this time.

Like so much in this networked, wired, connected world, these three signs of a different future are—and absolutely must be—interactive. They inform each other, they grow with each other, and they are connected! Together they provide a framework for a radical turnaround of The United Methodist Church in this century. It will not be easy and will not be a quick fix. We have been sinking into this mess for the better part of the last half-century. I suspect it will take God a few years of working on us, in us, and through us to refocus our energies and to teach the remnant to "take root downward, and bear fruit upward"—and outward. In what might be one of the most unlikely of places, I have been privileged to watch the stirrings of what that turnaround might look like. The Alabama–West Florida Conference is a statistical anomaly within The United Methodist Church: although the denomination has declined significantly over the last four decades, this area has grown. It has defied demographic logic, has survived devastating storms, has battled racism and poverty, and has grown and expanded its ministry locally and globally. It is, in no way, perfect; it has not arrived at the final destination; there is still work to be done on all fronts. This is a story of hope for the whole denomination. If God can accomplish it in this conference, it can be so anywhere. If it has been done here, why has it not been done in other areas? We are on our way, and the journey is incredible. The destination is even bolder. Together, we must "take root downward and bear fruit upward."

ACKNOWLEDGMENTS

From my earliest memories, books have been constant companions in my life. I am a reader, and I normally have at least two, if not three, books at my side, along with numerous journals and magazines. *Voracious* is a close but not altogether accurate description since I do find time to enjoy other activities. Through the forty or so books I read each year, I am being shaped and influenced by a whole host of other persons as I mark and inwardly digest what my eyes allow me to take in. Some of the ideas that are highlighted in this book have grown out of those encounters, although they have gone through numerous amendments, adaptations, and applications. Of this, I am well aware, and acknowledge that I have reshaped, tweaked, and merged suggestions of others out of my own experience of God and practice of leadership. In the last few years, several of my friends and partners in ministry have encouraged me to write a book. I have never pursued this ministry and discipline, although as a bishop I have written and shared messages regularly with the leaders of the conference to which I am appointed. I do it electronically, and some of those musings are preserved online in the archives section of the conference web site. It was with the encouragement of a few trusted friends to expand some of those reflections that led to the development of this manuscript. In reality this book has been taking shape over a number of years, has been through many revisions, has been spoken and discussed in a variety of settings, and now is in print for others to see. Thanks to those of you who provoked me into doing this, who believed I could do it, and who have encouraged me along the way.

As this book was in its genesis, I was privileged to have a conversation with Bob Ratcliff and John Kutsko at The United Methodist Publishing House in Nashville, Tennessee. They listened to my story and vision, the outline, and the early ideas and then, surprisingly, invited me actually to write a manuscript. They wanted to see more of those ramblings that initiated this work. I am very grateful to Dr. Ratcliff for his editing skills and for his many words of affirmation and encouragement.

Some of the initial themes that appear here came to me in an exchange of e-mails with longtime friend Lovett Weems, who now directs the Lewis Center for Church Leadership at Wesley Theological Seminary in Washington DC. Some of his research into the Alabama–West Florida Conference in comparison with other conferences prompted my reflecting and the writing of this book. Lovett was gracious enough to read an early draft of this manuscript and offer helpful insights, and for that I am grateful. Our Mississippi roots and Millsaps College student days continue to shape us both. Thanks, Lovett!

Paul Nixon was the Director of Congregational Development for the Alabama–West Florida Conference from 2002 until 2007. During that time he became a trusted friend and confidant as we worked together to nudge churches toward life and vitality, to plant new churches, and to strengthen clergy leadership skills. Paul has been a source of insight and inspiration for me, and I have learned much from him. In the summer of 2007, Paul moved to the Washington DC area where he is planting a multisite, multicultural congregation. He remains on my speed dial. Paul invested many hours of his time reading and reflecting with me on early drafts of this book. He has pushed me, challenged me, and encouraged me. Thanks, Paul, for your friendship and your passion for Jesus and for the church.

I am especially grateful to my wife, Deborah, who, since 1971, has been on this amazing journey with me. During the weeks that stretched into months while I wrote, edited, rewrote, and rearranged this document, she was patient and supportive (as always). She allowed me to take time to retreat to this computer when we might have otherwise done something together. Our two daughters are grown and no longer live with us, which certainly changes the dynamics and sounds of our home in Montgomery. When they come to see us—and especially when our two grandchildren are under our feet—the computer hibernates, and playtime surfaces. Even then, during the holiday season (with time out for our movies), they allowed me some space to continue writing. They are all—Deborah, Lucy, Amy and Eric, and now Amelia and Thomas—the joy of my life. God has richly blessed me!

Finally, none of this would have been possible without the people of the Alabama–West Florida Conference of The United Methodist Church. I dedicate this book to all of you with gratitude for your faithfulness in ministry, for extending the mission of Jesus in exciting and creative ways, for putting up with me and helping me as a rookie bishop learn something of this office, for taking the risks to incorporate into our life together some of my *flat world* and *flat organization* visioning and thinking, and for praying for me—I know you do because I feel it and know that we could not have done half of what we have accomplished for Jesus without that God-power. Thanks for being who you are, for evangelizing and making disciples, and for transforming the world— both in your neighborhoods and around the globe. I "always give thanks to God for all of you and mention you in [my] prayers, constantly remembering before our God . . . your work of faith and labor of love and steadfastness of hope in our Lord Jesus Christ" (1 Thess 1:2-3).

Pentecost 2007
—Larry M. Goodpaster

INTRODUCTION

We have an election!" With those or similar words, the announcement of an episcopal election came on the morning of July 13, 2000, at the Southeastern Jurisdictional Conference of The United Methodist Church. The reason I do not recall the exact words is simply that, to my utter amazement, my name followed immediately, and I was swept up in a range of emotions. The next days were filled with handshakes, congratulatory comments (usually coupled with tongue-in-cheek consolation), and plenty of advice-givers. There was also a great deal of anxiety as my wife and I faced the reality that we would be leaving friends and family in Mississippi—our home for all but twenty months of our twenty-nine years of marriage. Where would we be sent? How would we be received? What would be expected? On Friday evening, July 14, our curiosity was solved when we heard the assignment: the Alabama–West Florida Conference. We would be moving to Montgomery, Alabama, a city we knew little about except through its absolutely fascinating history. I knew a few people in the area, but it was, on the whole, a conference that I knew very little about even though it bordered the state and conference that had been my home for almost forty years. "This is a great conference," we heard again and again from the delegates and visitors who greeted us and welcomed us to our new home. What has amazed me as I have now lived and served in this area for more than six years is that, although greatness may be a relative assessment, the hope and excitement that is alive in this area is contagious. It is a hope that has not only transformed my view of the future for this one area but also given birth to possibilities for the whole of The United Methodist Church.

Whereas some geographic areas of the denomination have experienced minimal growth in membership, only a few can boast the kind of long-term, sustained growth that has characterized the churches of this particular conference. During the same thirty-five-year period (1970–2005) that The United Methodist Church in the United States *declined* by almost 25 percent, the Alabama–West Florida Conference *grew* by almost 20 percent. There were only two years during those thirty-five that the conference had a net loss of members. Worship attendance in the churches of the Alabama–West Florida Conference grew by 52 percent and the increases in stewardship and financial giving for the total ministry of the church was astronomical, even adjusted for inflation. During 2005, the churches that make up this area averaged sending six volunteers in mission teams every week somewhere in the world for short-term mission service. The churches also responded with record numbers of people who worked on disaster recovery teams in the wake of the hurricanes that ravaged this area in 2004 and 2005.

What is even more amazing is that this record of growth defies all normal demographic trends. This area of The United Methodist Church is composed of the southern tier of counties in the state of Alabama and the panhandle of the state of Florida. There is no major metropolitan area within the bounds of the conference. The two largest cities number less than 210,000 each. The migration of people from north to south has had some, but not dramatic, impact on the area. Most of this movement sends people farther south in the state of Florida, and even now, in the wake of the series of hurricanes, is sending many of them in a retreat northward toward the interior regions of the country. Some of the most sparsely populated counties and most economically deprived counties of the states of Florida and Alabama are located within the boundaries of what is known as the Alabama–West Florida Conference.

Yet in the last three decades of the twentieth century and the opening years of the twenty-first century, The United Methodist Church in this area grew in membership numbers, church vitality, mission outreach, and faithful stewardship. Now almost

150,000 United Methodist Christians are recorded as members of the 675 local churches. Given these statistics, given the demographics, and given the denominational culture of decline, why has the Alabama–West Florida Conference grown at a rate that is directly opposite that of the national church? Even more revealing is the fact that within the state of Alabama, the northern tier of counties, known as the North Alabama Conference, has followed the pattern of the rest of the denomination and declined in membership by 20 percent during the same time frame. Both conferences are located in the traditional Bible Belt, where growth might be expected. Yet one area has grown and the other declined.[1] Why has this occurred? What have been the factors contributing to the growth? What choices have been made that have led to a climate and expectation of growth as opposed to the denominational frustration of reporting annual declines in five figures?

This book has grown out of reflections and conversations with clergy and lay leaders of the Alabama–West Florida Conference. It is time to tell the story of one annual conference within The United Methodist Church that has shown sustained growth. It is time to offer hope to others who earnestly desire for the movement within the Wesleyan family known as United Methodism to reverse its decline. It is not always helpful, and is probably too late, for analyzing what went wrong and for placing blame at the doorstep of one group or another. In fact, we are all part of the same decline, and we all share in the responsibility for the slippery slope we are riding. The following pages will offer vision and hope, guidelines and principles, and choices and directions, and how those ingredients have been implemented within the Alabama–West Florida Conference. I will be among the first— and most vocal—to admit that the last thing needed in The United Methodist Church is for every annual conference to clone and become the Alabama–West Florida Conference. There are still too many crucial issues that must be addressed within this particular area to suggest that we have it all together or that we have achieved perfection.

We are, in good Wesleyan fashion, going on toward perfection, but we have not arrived. However, I do believe that the ethos that informs the corporate life of the churches of this annual conference can be caught, shaped, and practiced in other areas. This is not intended to be a book solely about us: do this and you will live! But this annual conference and this story do provide a background and some anecdotes and models that can point a way toward a different future for The United Methodist Church. Except for the distinctly Wesleyan theology that will be evident in the telling of this story, the principles discussed can be applied to other judicatories and adjusted for polity and guiding theological convictions, and I welcome that conversation. This is, however, primarily about The United Methodist Church, one judicatory leader, and an incredible collection of churches, individuals, and characters.

This is not a book about *me*. I have only had the good fortune to serve in this conference during the last seven years. Many of the patterns and growth standards were already established by the time of my arrival in Montgomery. I get to stand on the shoulders of other bishops who carved out a path: William Morris, C. W. Hancock, Lloyd Knox, Frank Robertson, Carl Sanders, and Kenneth Goodson. However, the observations, the recommendations, and the possibilities for the next thirty-five years are the result of my own study, reflection, experimentation, and application. I take responsibility for that, even as I give thanks for those who came before me. The people of the Alabama–West Florida Conference have been extremely patient and responsive, apprehensive and excited, inquisitive and supportive. Together we are charting a way into the future that may indeed hold some keys for the rest of the denomination—perhaps even for other members of the larger Body of Christ in the world. I am grateful for those who have read or listened to portions of this book over the last couple of years. Their insights, corrections, and provocations have focused my writing and thinking. But, at the end of the day, the book comes from my heart and soul, through my fingers pounding away at the keyboard of my omnipresent laptop computer.

CHAPTER ONE

CURRENT REALITY: A CRISIS IN THE MAKING

The quotation has appeared in a number of places, and with various renderings, but here is the version that Thomas Friedman cites in his insightful and significant book *The World Is Flat*. Lou Gerstner became the chief executive officer of IBM in 1992. Speaking to the Harvard Business School in 2002, Gerstner said, "Transformation of an enterprise begins with a sense of crisis or urgency."[1]

If The United Methodist Church is to be transformed in a way that recovers any semblance of the Wesleyan spirit out of which we were born, we must recognize, acknowledge, and confess that we are a denomination in crisis. Indeed, every historically mainline denomination finds itself in a similar position. For those of us in the Wesleyan tradition, we have lost any resemblance to the movement that affected England in the eighteenth century, that swept across the United States in the nineteenth century, and that spread like wildfire across Africa in the twentieth century. In America, we have managed to become what John Wesley feared: we have the form, we have the organizational structure, and we have the vocabulary, but we lack the power or the courage or the will to radically alter the downward spiral of membership and participation that will move us beyond surviving for a few more decades as a shell of our former self.

We have also managed to get tangled up in our own little worlds, to carve out our caves and corners into which we may retreat, and to choose sides in ways that divide us into parties that blame everyone else for the problems we have. The worst part of it is that there are too many United Methodists (both leaders and pew-sitters) who believe that we are doing just fine, that there is no crisis, and that we will somehow make it through. **Reality:** we are in a crisis. Without sounding like the comic character Chicken Little, who runs around shouting about a falling sky, I want to sound a note of urgency but quickly affirm that it is not a death sentence. Crisis gives us an opportunity either to throw in the towel and retreat or to lift our eyes and advance. We can hide under our collective steeples and await the end, or we can use the crisis as a breakthrough moment. What are some of the signs of the impending crisis that require our urgent, God-empowered attention and efforts?

1. MEMBERSHIP DECLINE

It has been well documented that The United Methodist Church is in a steep downward spiral in membership in the United States of America. In the last thirty-five years, the denomination has lost over 25 percent of its reported membership. When The Methodist Church and The Evangelical United Brethren merged in 1968, there were more than thirteen million members in forty-three thousand churches, and the decline that had already begun continued unabated. By 1970, membership stood at approximately 12.5 million. Thirty-five years later, at the end of 2005, The United Methodist Church counted less than eight million members in fewer than thirty-two thousand local churches. As a percentage of the total population of the United States, the church has declined to less than 3 percent. The church is in a free fall!

Even though The United Methodist Church has a church in almost every county of the country, the reality is that, for the most part, those individual franchises are declining and dysfunctional. They are operating out of a survival mode mentality. There are exceptions to such decline, and almost every state or annual conference can boast of at least a handful of United Methodist churches that are growing, healthy, and vital. Regrettably, there are not enough of those exceptions to offset the rapid decline of the whole. Even more regrettably, those churches that are growing are often treated by some denominational leaders with derision and skepticism. The prevailing wisdom goes that if some of our churches are growing there must be something wrong with them. Astounding! Either the leadership enjoys the death spiral, or it refuses to acknowledge that there is something wrong at the heart of the denomination. We may take some comfort in knowing that, at the present rate of decline, The United Methodist Church will close its last church in the United States in about ninety years. The "comfort" of that reality is that for most of us reading this paragraph in the first decade of the twenty-first century, that closing will not happen in our lifetime! We also take comfort in knowing that we are not alone in this decline. Those denominations traditionally called "mainline" or "mainstream" or "old line" flatlined years ago and are in as steep a decline as The United Methodist Church. Misery loves company! Since there are a few pockets of growth in every region, we also take some comfort in knowing that maybe a few buildings will be left standing and a remnant will be lingering in 2100! I am one of a growing number of bishops, denominational leaders, and others who are absolutely dissatisfied with this current reality and who are trying to lead in ways that will reverse the decline.

What does this downward spiral mean? Is it just a matter of losing members to death or other denominations? Is it a sign of bad record keeping, the zeal of the 1950s outrunning the accuracy of maintaining membership rolls? It seems that during my thirty-five years of ministry, most of our churches have been engaged in the practice known as "cleaning rolls" and "removing members." In fact, if we had spent as much time, energy, and compassion in reaching new generations as we have done in trying to find and contact long-departed members, we might actually have seen a reversal in the downward drift. Every person is important. Every member counts. This is why it is essential that we never lose sight of the fact that every "number" is a person loved by God, redeemed in Jesus, and gifted through the Spirit. No one should be lost or forgotten or neglected. But if the majority of our resources are directed toward maintaining the status quo rather than reaching the new, we will lose every time. This reality of membership decline *is* a crisis, and the urgency of the situation demands that action be taken. This reality of membership decline is also a sign that something is wrong deep inside the soul of the church; it is a symbol of the loss of enthusiasm and passion for those who are hurting, who are outside the Realm and Reign of God, and who have not heard, responded, or taken seriously the call of God in Christ Jesus. We have not fulfilled our calling as "ambassadors for Christ . . . God is making his appeal through us" (2 Cor 5:20).

2. LOSS OF INFLUENCE, LOSS OF VOICE

The decline is not simply about losing members; it is also about the loss of ratios: percentage of population, percentage of demographic growth, percentage of voters, or percentage of new generations. Statisticians thrive on such formulas and calculations. The steady decline in membership also signals a loss of influence within the life of individuals and communities. No longer does the institutional church, regardless of denominational label, shape society or determine office hours, shopping hours, or leisure hours. No longer does the Christian faith perspective influence the ethics, values, or behavior of the marketplace, the factory, or the boardroom. Is anyone listening? **Reality:** The United Methodist Church has no critical mass of people that can significantly shape or influence the culture. Our witness for Jesus is weakened as we argue among ourselves while the denomination crumbles around us. Attempting to adopt the ways of the culture in the name of being relevant waters down the gospel, compromises the faith, and does nothing to reshape the lives of people.

The world and its leaders are not hanging around the board-rooms, office suites, or break rooms awaiting a word from The United Methodist Church on what to do or how to do it. Yet we continue to operate out of a model in which we try to convince ourselves that everyone will sit up and take notice when we pass down our decrees. There is an extremely vital role for the voice of the prophet who calls into question the practices and philosophies that stand in direct opposition to the Reign of God. That vital message must be sounded in this century: hate evil, love good, and establish justice, which must roll down like waters (Amos 5:15, 24); do justice, love kindness, walk humbly with God (Micah 6:8). Resolutions, petitions, and symbolic meetings are ignored when the church itself is divided and in decline. Because of the continuing decline of membership, participation, and influence, we have lost our authoritative, authentic voice. We have lost our way.

3. AN AGING RANK AND FILE

Not only do the statistics reveal the continuing loss of members, they also reveal that The United Methodist Church is a "graying" denomination, with the average age of the church membership increasing annually, now well into their late fifties. At the other end of this spectrum, the number of members and participants under the age of thirty-five is dwindling. Little wonder that we tremble to know that the number of clergy under the age of thirty-five is becoming a small blip on the radar screen of Methodism since they are not in our congregations to begin with. We are getting old. We are growing weary and tired. For decades we told ourselves that the youth were the future of the church, but failed to do anything to excite or stir up the faith in them. *Reality:* Not only are we aging but we are also a denomination that has lost and is in the process of losing entire generations of people. A national "division" (church talk) on young adults might call attention to the issue and might propose elaborate schemes to reach those born after 1985, but, until the will of local churches matches the desire of generations, we will continue to grow old together.

4. IT IS THE TWENTY-FIRST CENTURY, PEOPLE!

One of the challenges facing annual conferences (judicatories) and bishops (denominational executives) in this twenty-first century is reflected in the dramatic shift that has taken place in the last four decades. During the same period of time that mainline denominations were rapidly decreasing in membership, participation, and influence, the world was undergoing massive change. The postmodern age is marked by the explosion of information, the proliferation of computer technology, relativistic individualism coupled with a pluralistic society, and the collapse of institutions built on the mid-twentieth century model of the industrial-militaristic philosophy. **Reality:** The world has changed! Dramatically! Too many churches still operate in the belief that we are still living in the 1950s!

I was a child in the 1950s and came of age in the 1960s, so I have been stamped and shaped by an era that ceased to exist long ago. I am of the generation that grew up with television. I well remember the first one my family brought into our home—it was absolutely fascinating. And choices: why we had three networks from which to pick our evening entertainment! We live in a world now where hundreds of choices are available every minute, where iPods and MP3 players multiply our choices, where the next generation of communication tools will soon make everything we know today obsolete at a pace that travels at warp speed. We live in a world where the laptop on which I am writing this sentence has more power, more capabilities, more speed, and more memory than the rooms full of computers only twenty years ago. We live in a world where, once a month, a computer somewhere in the world logs on to a satellite spinning deep in space, locks on to the computer chips implanted inside the automobile I drive, performs a diagnostic test sequence, generates a report on how this car is functioning, lists what maintenance attention I should give it, and delivers it to my e-mail address within minutes. I grew up in an era when one took the car to a local mechanic, who tinkered, tapped, and measured in order to discover a problem.

Sadly, too many of our churches and conferences are trying to function in this radically changed world out of an antiquated system. Too many still think that if we just work in the old system a little harder and longer, things will have a way of correcting themselves. Like the old shade-tree mechanic, we have tinkered and tapped our way into organizational charts that hinder the movement of God's Spirit. We have allowed the proliferation of agencies, commissions, and national events to continue on the theory that the more of these we have, the better we will be, the longer we will survive, the more faithful we will become, and the more difference we will make in the world.

5. A FRAGMENTED, HURTING WORLD

Even a casual reading of news articles following a national election in the United States is enough to reveal a divided country. If the people of the Christian faith are going to make a difference and contribute to making a different world, then we will have to recognize the deep fissures that exist and that surface primarily when conversation turns to politics and social issues. More than simply recognizing and acknowledging the fragmentation in our society, we cannot shy away from naming the issues (greed, self-centeredness, envy, and violence to start the list) and identifying the conflicts (broken relationships, suspicious and skeptical attitudes, and xenophobia to start another list). **Reality:** We live in a broken world where people are suffering and where hundreds of thousands of people are dying daily from preventable diseases that are directly tied to poverty or from militaristic power displays that devastate the land and that create a tragic category known as collateral damage. There are hurting people populating every corner of this country and of this planet.

Christian believers are called upon to witness to a different view of life and an alternative vision of the way life is to be lived in relation, in harmony, and in *shalom*. Yet, in our downward spiral, churches struggle to make a difference. There are glimpses of the generosity of the people called Methodists in response to the destructive powers of either nature or inhumanity. The outpouring of dollars and volunteers in response to the September 11, 2001, attacks, the tsunami in Southeast Asia in December 2004, and the hurricanes of 2004 and 2005, most particularly Katrina, was a sign of the possibility of what may yet be accomplished through the church. Such news-making events call attention to the pain and suffering of one moment in time. The reality is that the pain and suffering is a daily occurrence in much of the globe. Can The United Methodist Church offer spiritual and physical hope to a hurting world? If we continue our decline in the Western world, who will pick up the void that is left when we can no longer generate the dollars or the people?

6. THE VISION THING

Very few people doubt that the world has changed dramatically in the last half of the twentieth century and the first decade of the twenty-first century. We have lived through them all, and we will continue to wrestle with the changes that come toward us. Every organization and institution that has traversed the waters of uncertainty that these changes have brought has invested time and resources into developing mission and vision statements. If we can just figure out our purpose and our reason for existence, we will then find our way and know what we have to do to survive. Most United Methodists know and can quote ad nauseam the proverb about people perishing without a vision. **Reality:** Even though we have devised mission and vision statements, printed them in prominent places, and even memorized and recited them regularly, we are, as a denomination, drifting in the turbulent waters of this world. Although we boldly print that "the mission of the Church is to make disciples of Jesus Christ" (¶120, *The Book of Discipline*), we expend more energy trying to define it, argue about it, or work around it than actually doing it. We have lost any sense or awareness that the church does not *have* a mission, the church *is* a mission. The church is God's strategy for sharing, modeling, proclaiming, and living the gospel good news of Jesus, God's self-revelation of divine love for a hurting world and its people.

Daniel Wolpert has written about prayer practices and our life with God. In reflecting on some of the ancient writers and guides for the spiritual life, Wolpert makes this intriguing observation:

> Currently most churches are in flux and struggling in their attempt to define themselves in our so-called post-modern age. The days of the church as a center of social and community life are gone, and so congregations are groping about in the dark trying to decide if they are community centers, old-age homes, spiritual Wal Marts, or filling stations for the soul. This searching is made all the more difficult by the individualism permeating every aspect of our lives.[2]

In the chapters that follow, we will explore the implications of the current reality in which our denomination finds itself. Where will the vision that will energize and motivate us for the future emerge? How will we define ourselves and live into God's preferred future? What steps will be required of us to move from flux to faith, from decline to vitality, from groping about in the dark to galloping into the light of God's Reign, God's "kingdom come on earth as it is in heaven"?

The Alabama–West Florida Conference has struggled with these same realities, with the gospel of Jesus the Christ, and with the fresh movements of God's Spirit. We have not been immune from any of the realities of change that have affected all who live in this first decade of the twenty-first century and in this flat, well-connected world. Unlike much of the rest of the denomination, the Alabama–West Florida Conference has done so and yet found a way to post gains in membership, worship attendance, participation in God's mission, and generosity. We have discovered that the church, of all institutions, organizations, and entities, should not only understand but also lead the way in practicing what Jim Collins has named the Stockdale paradox. As defined in his ground-breaking best seller, *Good to Great*, this paradox is an important lesson to be learned and applied: "you must never confuse faith that you will prevail in the end—which you can never afford to lose—with the discipline to confront the most brutal facts of your current reality, whatever they might be."[3] I believe, and this book will illustrate, that the future of The United Methodist Church can be extremely bright, vital, and healthy. I believe, and from the experience of the Alabama–West Florida Conference am convinced, that The United Methodist Church can once again grow and demonstrate signs and wonders of God's grace for the entire world to see. There is a way. Are we willing to face facts? And do we have the will to follow?

TRANSFORMING HOPE

We are at a critical moment in the life cycle of what we know as The United Methodist Church. There is a sense of urgency that demands a creative response and, in John Wesley's terminology, holy living. This is a time that calls for critical thinking and reflecting, for building networks and for offering a word of hope to this world. It is a time to make hard choices about whether we will continue to be a strong voice for Wesleyan theology in the world and a major source for hope and healing in the lives of people who are hurting, lonely, confused, and uncertain.

This is not a time for any of us to point fingers or to blame the other. Easy targets are everywhere around us. Depending on which side of the theological spectrum one adopts, the easy target for the mess is the other extreme. Choosing sides over social issues only serves to foster an atmosphere of creating scapegoats and stereotypes. What is needed are signs of hope and evidence of health and vitality upon which we can build a radically different future. What is needed is to move beyond what we have known (it is no longer working) and how we have organized ourselves into a bureaucracy (it is inflexible, entrenched, and dead weight). What is needed is a vision that stirs and challenges us to live as faithful followers of Jesus. The kind of vision and hope that is needed is spelled out very well by Rosamund Zander and her husband, Benjamin Zander, in *The Art of Possibility*. They write, "A vision is a powerful framework to take the operations of an organization of any size from the *downward spiral* into the arena of possibility."[4] For us, that powerful framework is the hope that arises out of a different vision and different model, what Jesus proclaimed and modeled as the kingdom of God.

In a world of Roman occupation and oppression, Jesus embodied hope. In a time of institutional religious arrogance, Jesus proclaimed hope. To a people who were sick and tired, who were marginalized and estranged, Jesus was hope. This was a hope that transformed the lives of people, that redeemed and reconciled all of creation, and that revolutionized the world. It was a hope that generated a fresh vision and pointed toward an alternative worldview and way of living. It was a hope that inspired and encouraged.

John Wesley lived in interesting times. The Church of England was the dominant religious institution. It was moribund, routine, lifeless, and empty except for the rituals and the endorsement of the government to keep it going. John Wesley offered a message of hope to the masses who felt estranged from the religious leadership and the institutional organization of the church. John Wesley offered hope through the proclamation of a gospel that brought a renewed sense of mission and evangelism, and that provided a way to "flee from the wrath to come" (Matt 3:7). He broke with long established patterns of acceptability in order to transform society and to offer a different vision of church and what it may become.

We live in interesting times when what is needed once again is a vision of hope and healing that transforms lives, communities, and a world. There are those within the institutional church who would argue that our hope is to be found in what we already have. If we just shuffle the organizational chart one more time, if we give a little more money, if we chase after the next megachurch success story, if we travel the road of division and find an amicable way to separate ("just get rid of *them*")—then all will be well! When our hope is defined by what is wrong or by trying to do better, it ceases to be a transforming power. It is reduced to empty optimism or wishful thinking. It is void of any power of God flowing through us into a hurting church or a hurting world. "More of the same" is not hope—it is a method that produces the same results. "Stay the course" is not a transforming power—it is a recipe for a downward spiral.

As the book of Acts opens, Jesus tells the remaining handful of believers that they will receive power (Greek: *dynamis*). It is an intriguing possibility for us as well. The explosive power of God's Spirit changes everything; it re-creates everything; it gives birth to a movement that will eventually be named as *ecclesia* ("church"). Is it at all possible to be reclaimed by this power in the twenty-first century? I believe that, as Wesleyans, we United Methodists are well-positioned to think about connections and power sources. In a world that thrives on being wired and networked, we United Methodists understand (or should understand) "connection." In a world where power is misused and abused, we United Methodists can model a grace-induced power that is redemptive, constructive, and curative. Through a network (connection) of dynamic, God-empowered congregations, we could actually practice following Jesus faithfully and loving God and neighbor passionately. Such a vision of transforming hope could radically change the direction that our denomination and others are headed. Such hope can then transform not only our lives but ultimately also the world created and loved by God, yet broken and defaced by humanity.

Many individuals and groups, both inside and outside the church, have rediscovered a powerful verse from the prophet Jeremiah. It is found in a letter that Jeremiah sent to the leaders of the people who had been forced to live in exile from their homeland. It was a dark time for them. There was uncertainty and despair. If ever there was a crisis to live in and through, this was it. In the urgency of that moment, Jeremiah wrote, "For surely I know the plans I have for you, says the LORD, plans for your welfare and not for harm, to give you a future with hope" (Jer 29:11). It is from this verse that the 2008 General Conference of The United Methodist Church found its theme. If this is to be more than a onetime theme, then we cannot continue doing the same thing again and again. We must discover, live by, and embody a transforming hope that is grounded in God, who will always have a future. The only thing that remains is whether The United Methodist Church as it is currently configured will be part of that future.

CHAPTER TWO

CLICHÉS FOR MAINTAINING THE STATUS QUO

Patrick Lencioni, in his book *Silos, Politics, and Turf Wars*, describes what happens in many organizations, businesses, and institutions in the Western world today. Not surprisingly, his insights also describe what has also evolved within this denomination over the last half of the twentieth century. The church bureaucracy has built silos and engaged in an endless round of turf wars, protecting budgets and maintaining institutions rather than engaging the mission and vision with creativity and enthusiasm. Lencioni writes

> In most situations, silos rise up not because of what executives are doing purposefully but rather because of what they are failing to do: provide themselves and their employees with a compelling context for working together. . . . Pulled in many directions without a compass, they pursue seemingly worthwhile agendas under the assumption that their efforts will be in the best interest of the organization as a whole.[1]

The United Methodist Church has been pulled and pushed in so many directions over the last few decades it is amazing that we have survived at all. There has been nothing inherently wrong with any of the efforts, for every initiative, emphasis, and plan has addressed a significant need within our world. The critical issue has been that we have tried to do so many things that we have spread ourselves thin and stretched our dwindling resources. Our turf wars have resulted in a regular battle over who gets what share of the budget and the monies that are funneled to the general church. We have hesitated to call our current reality a crisis because the dollars continue to flow, in ever increasing amounts, but in ever decreasing percentages of available wealth. We have not sensed the urgency of the moment because the institution remains in tact, the bureaucracy expands and digs in, and thousands of people still show up for a worship service every week.

Lencioni pushes us. A recurring theme in *Silos, Politics and Turf Wars* is the necessity of a crisis to move us to action. In fact, he argues, that in order for real change to occur in any organization or institution, a crisis must occur. He even suggests that "a crisis brings out the best in companies."[2] Even more challenging, he goes a step further: "Why wait for a crisis. . . . Why not create the same kind of momentum and clarity and sense of shared purpose that you'd have if you were on the verge of going out of business?"[3] As a pastor for more than thirty-five years, and now as a bishop since 2000, I have watched the gradual eroding of our denomination. I believe we are in a crisis, and there is an urgent need for a response that will reverse our trends, restore our confidence, rebuild our reputation, and reignite our influence for God in the world. I lament the setting in which I am called upon to lead during these first decades of the twenty-first century. However, I also know that there are others who do not believe we are in crisis mode yet. So, with Lencioni, I would urge us (laypeople and clergy, bishops and pastors, general agency staff and bureaucrats, baptized followers of Jesus Christ) to at least act as if we were and create an exciting new momentum forward.

Unfortunately, whether at the local church level or the broader, general church level, calls for renewal, revolution, or repositioning are met with skepticism, denial, and hostility. The deck seems stacked in favor of the tried and the tired, and the silos and turf boundaries that have been erected. We do not look with favor upon those who rock the boat, who offer alternative views of the future, or who suggest there is a crisis that must be faced. It has not always been that way within our Methodist family. With John Wesley, our life began as a movement to renew an institution, but then gradually became an institution. Can an institution become a movement again? Can we recover some of the early fervor that inspired John Wesley, drove Francis Asbury, and birthed a denomination? We have plenty of excuses of why and how we got to where we are. If you listen carefully, you will hear them in the sermons, the writings, the pronouncements, the articles, and the messages that surface frequently throughout Methodism. Listen to the voices that would hold us back, offer excuses, and hinder any renewal movement or revolutionary action.

I WOULD RATHER BE FAITHFUL THAN SUCCESSFUL

I never cease to be astonished by this excuse. It has a way of suggesting that it is perfectly fine to be in a downward spiral, and that those congregations in the two or three growing areas and conferences are somehow to be dismissed. The underlying assumption is that it is impossible to be both faithful and successful. In the grand Wesleyan tradition in which we stand, this must be a *both/and* conversation, not an *either/or* choice. In fact, if one is being faithful to the gospel, faithful to following Jesus, faithful to loving God and neighbor, and faithful to the power of grace active in life, then the results will be revealed in growth, health, and vitality.

The tendency in our Western society is to define success strictly in terms that can be counted and measured. We like to keep score, to gauge success by how big we grow or by how large our asset base may be. In that sense, such an excuse as this one may be legitimate and call into question what we are doing and why. If our only purpose is to grow a church, and beat out our neighbors, then we have drastically misread the call of Christ to follow him. However, it is also the case that what we measure and count are the very things that we value, get our attention, and energize our efforts. When we are held accountable for sharing the grace-news of what God has done in Christ, then we will be attentive to those who have opted out of church or never received an invitation to join. In the world of retail, twenty-first-century technology has made it possible to count, measure, and evaluate what is happening hourly. Computers speed calculations on how well a store has done in the last hour (number of customers, average sales, volume of items purchased) compared to other stores in a region, or compared to the same hour of the same day last month or last year, and, most important, compared to the established hourly or daily goal.

This is not to suggest that the church should follow suit and mimic such transactions and calculations. What is disturbing, however, is that we assume that all counting is bad and that the continued downward spiral is acceptable. After all, we tell ourselves, we are being faithful and that means fewer and fewer people will want to come along. Citing John 6, where some people refuse to go any further with Jesus, we conclude that we are off the hook when it comes to adding, counting, and expanding the number of people who are part of the journey within and toward the Reign of God. The book of the Acts of the Apostles tells quite a different story.

If we read Acts from the perspective of being faithful, rather than successful, then those who follow the Way (Acts 9:2), later to be called Christians (Acts 11:26), who assembled themselves into the *ecclesia* (church) would not have existed beyond the first chapter. After all, if they were *only* going to be faithful, that handful of believers, the 120 who were counted (Acts 1:15), would have elected Matthias and stopped right there. They were being faithful to what Jesus had done—called and worked with twelve—end of story. They could have opted to keep replacing that twelfth person as age or death caught up with each one in turn, and enjoyed their small fellowship where everyone knew all their names. Or, if they were *only* going to be faithful, the story might have ended at Acts 15, the first great council of the church. The Jerusalem factor would have prevailed,

> "That we never forget that we are serving Jesus Christ. That it is not for our own glory or personal accolades, although it is nice to be remembered. We are the church because we love God and because we love each other." (Chip Hale, Spanish Fort United Methodist Church, Spanish Fort, Alabama)

and the spread of the faith through the preaching of Paul and Barnabas and others to, of all people, Gentiles, would have ended. They would have been faithful to their heritage and remained a sect, and a rather small one at that.

But Acts is an explosive collection of twenty-eight chapters, where the Spirit of God moves into the hearts, souls, lives, and actions of the people who were faithful and sends them into the world with a dynamic message of hope, healing, and salvation through faith in Jesus the Messiah. They were *both* faithful *and* successful. In response to the gospel and in the power of the Spirit, they hit the streets and reported thousands of converts in response to the good news of Jesus. They faithfully told the story, proclaiming the name of Jesus, repeating it time and time again, and allowing that story to shape their lives, move them beyond the confines of their small mindedness, and to expand the numbers of persons actively involved in the faith through *ecclesia*. They were faithful to the call to serve (Acts 6) and faithful to the call to witness for and about Jesus (Acts 1:8). And they were successful—enormously successful, as thousands were added to their number daily, weekly, and annually.

Today, there can be no better model for how we practice being church than the book of Acts. Faithfulness and success should be seen as two acts of the same play, with one theme running through the entire work: "This Jesus is 'the stone that was rejected by you, the builders; / it has become the cornerstone.' There is salvation in no one else" (Acts 4:11-12a). Interestingly,

> **"I long for the day that The United Methodist Church will be known for our missional spirit and commitment to scriptural holiness."** (Larry Bryars, Shalimar United Methodist Church, Shalimar, Florida)

this bold statement from Peter comes in the aftermath of a healing. We are called to serve God in hundreds of ways: providing food, visiting the sick, sitting with the lonely, embracing the forgotten ones, extending medical and healing care, practicing grace. But in that service—in our faithful response to the claim of God on our lives—we are also called to be successful; that is, telling the story so that those who have never heard will hear and respond; so that those who have turned away, burned out, drifted aside, or missed out hear good news proclaimed and discover the joy of life with God. As we are faithful, people will respond, and churches will grow. To excuse ourselves by asserting that we are faithful and have no desire to be counted as successful is to miss an important dimension of the gospel.

The Alabama–West Florida Conference has a number of churches that have caught a glimpse of what it means to be *both* faithful and successful. Some of the largest churches of the denomination can be found within the borders of this annual conference: Frazer Memorial United Methodist Church in Montgomery, Alabama; Christ United Methodist Church in Mobile, Alabama; Gulf Breeze United Methodist Church outside Pensacola, Florida; Niceville United Methodist Church in Niceville, Florida; and the First United Methodist Churches of Montgomery, Auburn, and Dothan, Alabama, and Pensacola, Florida. Every one of those churches exceed one thousand in worship attendance, show growth annually, and are actively engaged in faithful service among the poor, the marginalized, the hungry, and the lonely. They demonstrate in the community and around the world that as churches reach out in service to others, people are attracted and respond to giving themselves away, sharing their resources, and serving God.

WE ARE JUST ABOUT THE RIGHT SIZE

This statement is most often uttered by well-meaning church members whose congregation stopped growing and reaching out to neighbors decades ago. Consequently, the congregation has turned in on itself, has determined that its primary purpose is to keep the doors open one more year, and has decided that enjoying each other's company is a value that outweighs faithfully extending the gospel. For the most part, these congregations have become quaint chapels or convenient preaching stations and are so satisfied with the status quo that just about any person standing in the pulpit is sufficient.

Somewhere along the way those who live by this value statement have determined that "community" means "small," where what happens at the church can be easily managed and controlled. Community must go deeper than simply knowing everyone who sits in the pew on a Sunday morning. It must be broader than simply the four walls that mark the boundaries of a building. When a congregation turns inward and rejects or neglects an outward focus, the church has made a conscious decision for a slow death, in the name of "community" and "being the right size." These churches have chosen the path of being neither faithful in service and ministry to others nor successful in reaching new people, especially new generations of people. For a church to be a community, it must come together around a common purpose that emerges from what it means to be the Body of Christ. *Being the right size* or *being family* are not terms synonymous with being the Body of Christ.

During the 1990s, the Council of Bishops of The United Methodist Church was engaged in an initiative focused on children and poverty. For many churches and conferences, this initiative galvanized their ministry and refocused their energies around a common purpose. The last document produced by the council for this initiative was given the title "Our Shared Dream: The Beloved Community." It was in that document that the bishops spelled out what such a community, a Body of Christ, might look like. This kind of community emerges when "love of God and faith in Christ are expressed in selfless love for all the peoples of the world. This requires a complete turning away from each religiosity."[4] The bishops continued in that document with this description of the community: "a dramatic sign of the presence in the world of the spirit of Jesus Christ, in which the walls of separation are broken down so that all—Jew and Gentile, male and female, young and old, slave and free, rich and poor, those near and those far away—may be one."[5] Those churches that opt for the "right size" mentality are choosing the way of easy religiosity, finding comfort in their smallness, and refusing to be a dramatic sign of God's presence in the world. After all, if we do that, the reasoning goes, others may start showing up and then we would not know everyone. Before you know it, we will no longer be the right size.

Every annual conference within Methodism is overrun with small membership churches, often running as high as two-thirds of all the churches in a region. Every annual conference is then faced with the task of supplying pastors to take care of those small membership churches. An inordinate amount of time and resources are directed toward those congregations that are, at best, on life-support and waiting out the inevitable. And every annual conference allows it to continue! The challenge, as will be discussed in chapter 4, is to assist local churches in catching a different vision, walking a different path, and moving from "right size" thinking to thriving and flourishing, healthy and growing.

WE'RE HAPPY JUST THE WAY WE ARE!

This is a variation of the previous excuse, but deadly in that when a congregation grows happy or content or satisfied, there is little incentive to change. In those situations where status quo has become the preferred way of being, any attempt to initiate different worship patterns, creative outreach ministries, or alternative class meeting times is met with derision and dismissal. No one should be happy that a local church is declining, but we excuse ourselves by declaring that we are a happy family and then blocking any attempts to engage in practices that will expand the family. Just as potent at every level of the institutional church, the spirit of this phrase stifles creativity and flexibility, and perpetuates a system that may have been effective at one point in time, but no longer has the power to affect the world or the church.

A parallel mantra often accompanies this excuse: *if it ain't broke, don't fix it.* Those in leadership roles often find themselves managing the system and believing that everything is going to work out fine. The current reality is that the system, if not already broken, is stretched so thin that it is about to snap. Attempts to shuffle or redesign the system and the organization are met with resistance because it is not perceived as being broken and what we really need is more cooperation—and more money! Between the turf wars that rage among general agencies, the suspicion that exists among local church members, the ineffectiveness of many of the clergy and the disagreements and arguments that surface over theology, Christology, and Scripture— the system is not working!

When I arrived as bishop in the Alabama–West Florida Conference in September 2000, I found an area that was growing in membership, but with a great deal of complacency and self-satisfaction. Outwardly and by the numbers, the conference was doing well! Inwardly we lacked a cohesive vision and common purpose. Organizationally, we were trying to function with a system that had been perpetuated for decades. During the next four years, we made some critical decisions that have reshaped and reinvigorated the life of the conference and pointed it in a new direction. We broke the system and began reshaping our work so that we could continue and expand our growth trends and be an expression of the Reign of God in our lives, through our churches, and into the world. In a spirit of continuous improvement, we knew that we could not be satisfied with the status quo nor with resting on our past achievements. As in the

> "Long-term healthy leadership creates a healthy church, which enables growth, creativity, stability, and enables a leader to lead with vision. This long-term leadership in the local church could only happen in our United Methodist Church structure with bishops who support it." (Cory Smith, Woodland United Methodist Church, Montgomery, Alabama)

life cycle of any organization we were in a strategic moment to be reborn and to reinvent ourselves for future growth and vitality.

Our work began with an eighteen-month discernment process in which we caught a vision of what we were going to be about at the conference level: *creating healthy, dynamic, thriving congregations*. Growing out of that vision, we then redesigned our conference organization to turn the resources away from institutional survival to congregational health. We replaced the old Conference Council on Ministries with a Conference Leadership Team that we named our CORE Team ("Connecting Our Resources and Empowerment Team"). We reduced the number of conference boards and committees, and yet tended to all of the disciplinary mandates that are required of us in our current bureaucratic system. We redefined the responsibilities and role of the district superintendents, focusing on coaching and consulting more than administrative paper-pushers. We chose to limit the number of conference-level committees on which the superintendents serve in order to free their time and energy to focus on developing the local church and the clergy leaders in their respective districts. To emphasize this new day, we reduced the number of districts— not for financial reasons but for signaling this new way of leading and providing resources to congregations. We initiated conversations about clergy effectiveness and congregational health, understanding that the two are integrally connected. We continue to plow new ground, to break old habits, and to encourage, provoke, and inspire clergy and laity to build healthy churches that are both faithful and successful, that are both inwardly and outwardly focused, and that are practicing the means of grace to be the Body of Christ.

We are doing things that have never been done before, and there has been resistance; those who were happy have been dissatisfied with many of the changes. Along the way we have stumbled, we have revisited and reshaped some decisions, and we have sought always to be open to the movement of God's Spirit in our actions and ministry. It is a model based on the book of Acts, where new ways of doing things were popping up daily. Is there hope for the denomination as a whole? Can we move in new directions that will radically reshape how we go about the business of being church and becoming the Body of Christ in the twenty-first century? The reality is that if we have any hope of doing so, we cannot keep doing business the way we have always done it.

IF YOU KEEP DOING THE SAME THING, YOU WILL GET THE SAME RESULTS

How many times have leaders, lay and clergy, in churches and parachurch organizations recited this phrase? We know it is true. Yet it appears that we have no energy, no willpower, no resolve to do anything differently. We have been down a number of roads in an effort to get different results. Some have embraced the church growth literature, others have attempted total quality management, and still others have sold out to a marketplace culture. In recent years, some have been watching, listening, and imitating the emergent church movement. All the while, others (a majority?) keep doing the same thing that they have always done and seem to be surprised or not bothered by the fact that we keep getting the same results: declining membership and participation, dwindling financial support, and frustration and despair. What is called for is a radical renewal—a revolution if you will—of the connection. If we know that we will get the same results, then we should also know that in order to turn the corner and reverse the direction we must stop doing some things and start doing others. That is the rub! Learning what to say no to is the critical issue because each group or agency or board believes it has the inside track on what is wrong and what is needed to correct the course.

Even this book becomes yet another in a long list of books and articles about what needs to happen to reverse the decline and recover the original passion and compassion that drove the Methodist movement. Over the last twenty years, a number of writers, visionaries, and church leaders have been published by The United Methodist Publishing House addressing concerns and directions. In 1986, Richard Wilke's *And Are We Yet Alive* sounded themes for the church to address for its "future." This was followed the next year by a collaborative effort by William Willimon and Robert Wilson, *Rekindling the Flame*, outlining "strategies" for the denomination to follow. That same year (1987) *Facts and Possibilities*, written by Douglas Johnson and Alan Waltz, suggested an "agenda" for the church. By 1995, an idea for "reforming" the church was put forth by Andy Langford and William Willimon in *A New Connection*. Lyle Schaller weighed in on the subject ten years later with his book *The Ice Cube Is Melting* (2004). All of these, and others like them, have initiated discussions resulting in some tinkering with the system. Add this one to the list, but this time from the perspective of one who happens to be serving in an area where there are many healthy, growing congregations, and where an entire conference has shown steady, sustained growth over three decades. Shall we keep doing the same thing? Are we satisfied with the same results? Regrettably some are. I am not.

SO WHERE DO WE GO FROM HERE?

Current reality stares us in the face, with the future promising more of the same unless some new directions are taken.

Remember the Stockdale paradox from the first chapter: face the brutal facts of current reality, but never lose faith. I am not alone in holding firmly to the belief that in the end the church will prevail because the church is of God. That is why we can learn lessons and principles from the secular literature of organizational theories and business models, but not be totally dependent upon them for the church. We are of a different spirit—the Spirit of God. That is why the lessons, models, and principles from the book of Acts are applicable even in the twenty-first century. That is why we must return to our roots and our Wesleyan heritage. There is hope and power in the vision, wisdom, and insights of John and Charles. There must be a continual rediscovery of Wesleyan theology and ecclesiology.

It is customary for the general secretaries of the several general agencies within The United Methodist Church to present an address in the course of the regular board meetings of the directors. Since 1996 I have had the opportunity to serve on three different such agencies: the General Commission on Religion and Race (1996–2000, prior to my election as a bishop), the General Board of Church and Society (2000–2004), and, currently, the General Board of Global Ministries, so I have heard my share of them. For the most part, these addresses highlight the recent work of the agency and outline the next major efforts or concerns that must be faced. Even though I was not present, I received a printed copy of the address delivered by Sandra Lackore, General Secretary of the General Council on Finance and Administration, in November 2006. The title of her presentation was "Changing the Wind" and opened with this assessment:

> I believe our Council and our Church are at a crucial moment in our history. It is critical for all of us as Church leaders to take notice of our surroundings, to name what we see and feel, and fully engage in what I believe is a pivotal point for our denomination. I do believe that God is doing a new thing within our denomination. Like the wind of hope over the earth in the creation story, the spirit of God is hovering over us and creating a wind of change.[6]

I believe she has named where we are and what is a hope that is swirling around this denomination. The issue is whether those of us in leadership positions, and those who are part of the rank-and-file members of local congregations named United Methodist will feel and catch the wind and become the agents and catalysts for changing the direction of the denomination.

In the paragraph that followed those introductory statements, Lackore quotes at length a passage from *God's Politics* by Jim Wallis. In a provocative passage, Wallis likens politicians to people who stick their fingers in the air to determine the direction of the wind and then head off in that direction. Let me also quote Wallis's next statements at length. His words bear hearing and pondering.

> The great practitioners of real social change, like Martin Luther King, Jr. and Mahatma Gandhi, understood something very important. They knew that you don't change a society by merely replacing one wet-fingered politician with another. You change society by *changing the wind*. Change the wind, transform the debate, recast the discussion, alter the context in which political decisions are being made and you will change the outcomes. Move the conversation around a crucial issue to a whole new place, and you will open up possibilities for change never dreamed of before. You will be surprised at how fast the politicians adjust to the change in the wind.[7]

Whatever proposals may be heard through the writing and reading of this book, it is my intent to change the conversation. Is it the right move or the correct topic? That will remain for others to decide. For me and for the conference in which I presently serve, the choices that have been made have resulted, and continue to result, in growing churches, congregations moving from merely surviving to thriving, and both faithful and successful models of service and ministry. This is not a call for another effort at changing the structure of The United Methodist Church, although I am not sure we can survive if we do not radically change. Paul Borden has named the issue squarely: "The creation of new structures will never produce renewal in an organization.

Renewal is instigated with a new mission, a compelling vision, and the adoption of new values."[8]

Renewal in The United Methodist Church will mean bringing into existence a system that is in harmony with our Wesleyan heritage and theology and that takes into account the twenty-first century world in which we live and move and have our being. It is a system with several components, all of which must work together for the good of the whole. It is a system that encourages effective clergy leadership, which cultivates and motivates vital, thriving congregations that embrace change in the Spirit and power of God and that offer hope, healing, and hospitality for a hurting world. In order to implement (and improve) this system, there are some conscious choices that conferences, bishops, and other leaders will have to make in order to make a difference and shape a renewed denomination. I will offer some hints at what steps could be taken that will alter our path, change the wind, and produce different results. The ingredients are effective clergy leadership, thriving congregations, innovative outreach, a constant rediscovery of the Wesleyan heritage, and a refocused leadership.

CHAPTER THREE

LEADERSHIP! LEADERSHIP! LEADERSHIP!

The church claims leadership as a gift of God to the church, as due to the leading of God. Jesus did not accomplish his work in the world on his own, but appointed the Twelve to aid him in forming his followers and doing the work of the kingdom of God.[1]

In the latter writings of the New Testament, it is clear that the leadership of the new creation called *ecclesia* would rest in the hearts, hands, and lives of those named as pastors. The task and vocation of a pastor in this present time, as in that ancient time, is a challenging one and is not to be undertaken as a career of last resort or as something one wants to try out for a season. Reflecting on the passage quoted above, I have come to believe that to serve as a pastor is to know that one is (1) inspired, called, and led by God; (2) on a journey with Jesus; (3) to equip others to be faithful followers; and (4) to do Kingdom work in this present time. To be a pastor in the twenty-first century is, at the very least, to embody these four characteristics and to understand them as interrelated. No one part can be separated from the others. No one part can be singled out as more important than the others. This chapter is specifically about clergy leadership and the unique way we are called to live out our faith-response to God.[2]

I served two years as a district superintendent in the Mississippi Conference and have now served as a bishop since 2000. I have observed, and can with confidence conclude, that effective clergy leadership is the single most important and determining factor in the health of a congregation. That does not diminish the role of partnerships and teamwork with laity. That does not in any way take from the significant ministry of the thousands of laypeople who are engaged as faithful followers, witnesses, and servants of Jesus every day. It does, however, emphasize the importance of the task of equipping and preparing all people for the work of ministry. We must understand that we are in this together, and that we cannot do any of the work of ministry on our own. As Willimon accurately points out, Jesus did not accomplish his work alone, but rather called to himself a small group of believers and followers whom he equipped and prepared for ministry that reached beyond one particular locale. That mantle was taken up in the book of Acts where we read again and again of partnerships and teams of people doing God's work in the world: Peter *and* John, Paul *and* Silas *and* Timothy *and* Barnabas *and* Luke *and* Priscilla *and* Aquila and on it goes.

In the Alabama–West Florida Conference, as in every other region of The United Methodist Church, we devote a great deal of time building and enhancing these partnerships in ministry. No church in this present age will become healthy and grow without the vital link of relationship and collaboration of lay and clergy for the sake of Jesus Christ. Unfortunately, this is not always the case, and great conflicts arise when either lay or clergy start to believe that they are the key components of the entity we call church. Too often well-meaning people (lay and clergy) wind up on opposite sides, struggling with each other for control and command. Creative partnerships must be forged, nurtured, and lived out if the church is to be the Body of Christ and is to do kingdom business on earth. How do we go about doing that? It starts with baptism and the acknowledgment that every baptized believer is a minister, and every baptized believer has a ministry. It is out of that body of believers and baptized followers that some people are called and led out by God to serve sacramentally in

> **"We need to be the light of hope and salvation to a lost world. We need ones to move from their personal agendas to discovering what God's agenda should be for the church, because the church in many places has lost the real power of God's grace and mercy."** (Steve Rascoe, Park Memorial United Methodist Church, Troy, Alabama)

the world, for the church, and by grace and in the power of God's Spirit. All clergy must remember that we are, first of all, baptized and a part of the *ecclesia*. Our calling and credentialing does not elevate us to positions where we lord it over the laity. Rather, our calling invites us, challenges us, and identifies us as those who "equip the saints for the work of ministry, for building up the body of Christ" (Eph 4:12). All of us together are "ambassadors for Christ," entrusted with the ministry of reconciliation (2 Cor 5:16-21).

Let me say it again: partnerships are vitally important to the health and growth of the church and the extension of God's mission and our ministry to all people wherever they may live. However, it is the issue of clergy effectiveness that is and must be a major piece in any strategic makeover of the whole Methodist connection. I am convinced that the future of this movement known as Methodism is contingent upon developing excellent, effective leaders, who will serve as pastors of churches, who will inspire and equip all baptized believers for the work of ministry, and who will build up the Body of Christ. I am equally convinced that, in many cases, it will be the laity who will ignite the flame that will transform mediocrity into excellence and status quo into soaring faithfulness. After all it was, in large measure, laypeople who planted Methodism on American soil and led it to its amazing expansion serving as class leaders and exhorters, who told the story, formed disciples, and planted churches. Together, we will make a difference and make a different church.

37

EXCELLENCE IN MINISTRY

Across The United Methodist Church and other major denominations and configurations of the Body of Christ on earth, there are numerous conversations centered on the issue of clergy effectiveness. In some ways, we know what it is when it is being fulfilled, but describing it, defining it, and detailing characteristics of it has become a daunting task. With other leaders across the church, I have been in more conversations centered on the issue of *ineffectiveness* and on what to do about those pastors who are unable to successfully, artfully, or personally build up the Body of Christ. I have also listened to the yearning for quality, excellent leaders for every size church on the map, from local church pastor-parish relations committees to boards of ordained ministry.

In his book *Deep Change*, Robert Quinn writes, "Reaching a level of excellence involves analyzing each individual situation and determining what is right. It entails good communication, cooperation, high expectations, risk, and trust."[3] Quinn's categories give us a starting point to think about effectiveness and to pursue excellence in pastoral leadership—not for selfish reasons, not for personal career advancements, and not for the next move to a larger church. We understand that each congregation is unique, each has its own set of unwritten expectations and dreams, and each has its own vision of how it will live into the mission of the church—that big, broad, all-encompassing mission to make disciples of Jesus Christ, as *The Book of Discipline of The United Methodist Church* identifies it. We are called to focus our attention on encouraging, developing and utilizing God-granted skills on behalf of God for the sake of the mission and the vitality of the church. Across the Alabama–West Florida Conference, we hope to develop a critical mass of excellent clergy leaders, who in turn will inspire others to move forward. We also know that, again quoting Quinn, "The land of excellence is safely guarded from unworthy intruders. At the gates stand two fearsome sentries—risk and learning. The

> **"I believe the key to reversing our denominational decline (including, of course, the work and power of the Holy Spirit) is the *quality* and *effectiveness* of the person appointed to lead. . . . Very few churches will be able to rise above the effectiveness level of their leader and pastor."** (Jeff Spiller, Christ United Methodist Church, Mobile, Alabama)

keys to entrance are faith and courage."[4]

To be a pastor is to be caught up in a vocation, that is, a calling that is at its heart a response to God's grace, love, and invitation. Before it is anything else that we do (any book we read, course we take, or degree we earn), ordained, licensed, or commissioned, ministry is something God initiates. It is all about grace, which is why 2 Corinthians 4:1-17 is such a critical passage for the life of a clergy leader. The images literally leap out of that passage: "we do not lose heart . . . we do not use deception . . . we do not preach ourselves . . . we are hard pressed." Yet, there is grace; there is always grace. From Paul's point of view, we are all just clay pots on a shelf. Some might even suggest that we are just a bunch of cracked pots, living out our days in some fanciful dream either of past or future glory. But the surprise of it all is this: God chose to place within these earthen vessels a treasure. God decided that the way the treasure would become visible in the world was to get the clay pots off the shelf and into the world through the church. All of this, Paul says, is to show that the power belongs to God and not to us.

This vocation, if it is to be authentic, seeks us. It is not a career, in that we did not choose it on our own. It is not a job where our daily chores have been outlined for us by superiors. It is not even a profession, where certain skills can be taught and learned, and a paycheck received. In responding to God, we understand that the gospel is something that is to be lived out, that is to be embodied and incarnated in the world through people. "Our only hope is to cling to our vocation, to adhere to the sense that God has called us, rather than ourselves, that God has a plan and purpose for how our meager efforts fit into God's larger scheme of things. God's vocation is the only ultimate validation of our ministry."[5] With that sense of being called and of claiming ours as a vocation, it should become an earnest desire to serve with excellence, to lead effectively, and to build up the Body of Christ to the best of our ability under the guidance of the Spirit and by the grace of God.

What is called for then is to motivate, inspire, and equip clergy in the grand tradition and heritage of John Wesley. From the beginning of the Methodist movement in England, Wesley's practice, his theology, and his understanding of the Christian life within a class, band, society, or church was predicated on effective leaders. The word *effective* is obviously a more Americanized word that has only come into our vocabulary in the context of leadership. Wesley had a different question that focused around the same concerns: *Have they fruit?* In other words, is there evidence of God's grace showing up in the results of their ministry and leadership in a community? It seems obvious that for Wesley that any sign of ineffectiveness—any failure to bear fruit—any sign of weakness or failure resulted in a weakened witness to and for Jesus and ultimately in a weakened church and connection. Bearing fruit, for Wesley and for us, must not simply be about those items we can measure by counting. To bear fruit is to be intimately linked with God's love for us, our love for God, and our love for our neighbor. According to Jesus we are to *abide* in his love (John 15) as a sign of fruit bearing ministry.

In February 1756, Wesley wrote "An Address to the Clergy," which should still be required reading for pastors at least annually. In this address, he describes some of the characteristics and responsibilities that are to be exhibited among the clergy. It is a lengthy document, filled with the phrases and perceptions of the eighteenth century (particularly male-dominated language) but

> "Our system does not encourage entrepreneurial leaders, or even strong leaders, to enter the ministry. That must change. Much needs to change, but above all, we must become dependent on [Jesus]. God raised up the Methodist movement and empowered it . . . and is the only one who can breathe the spiritual life into our churches that will cause us to reach people . . . then we will see life and growth."
> (Ralph Sigler, Harvest United Methodist Church, Dothan, Alabama)

also filled with insights and wisdom for service in our time. One of the first of a whole list of expectations: "Ought not a Minister to have . . . a good understanding, a clear apprehension, a sound judgment, and a capacity of reasoning with some closeness?"[6] Wesley believed this was first because the clergy must be able to understand and care for those who are within the context and community where he or she is sent. He continues, "Is it not highly expedient that a guide of souls should have likewise some liveliness and readiness of thought?"[7] Then follows a long list of needed "endowments," which a clergy was (and is) expected to learn. Not the least of these for this present age: "No less necessary is a knowledge of Scriptures, which teach us how to teach others."[8] For Wesley, as for us, these gifts and skills are both inherently present and are acquired, both a gift from God and our gift back to God as we develop, mature, and increase our skills and abilities. Have you been equipped by grace for the task that is before you? And are you willing to learn more in order to enhance those gifts? Our willingness to serve and our effectiveness as clergy begins with our relationship with God and continues as that relationship grows and as we grow in our skills that produce fruit for the glory of God and the building up of the church.

TWENTY-FIRST-CENTURY PASTORAL LEADERSHIP

In recent years the amount of material being produced on the subject of leadership has expanded expeditiously. It seems that we have become obsessed with the topic, perhaps because there is a pervasive feeling that there is a severe shortage of leaders in every walk of life. Most of those persons held up as models for great leadership are, in many ways, larger than life. The circumstances and their successes are in very different times or organizations from those faced by clergy who are sent to lead local churches. We may learn some principles from Attila the Hun or Abraham Lincoln or John Wooden or Jack Welch—but the setting in which we are called upon to lead is radically different. It is time to learn and apply some lessons for pastoral leadership in the church!

LEADERSHIP LESSON ONE

A leader in and for the church is a committed follower of Jesus. Although we can profit from the previously mentioned writers or from others such as Jim Collins, Margaret Wheatley, Edwin Friedman, Stephen Covey, or Ken Blanchard, there is no way to underestimate the absolute necessity of, first of all, being a disciple of Jesus Christ. This should go without saying but bears emphasizing as lesson one. Called out from among the baptized followers of Jesus, the clergy learn to lean on and trust God from the very beginning. When or if the clergy moves out on her or his own, attempting to function separate from the identity that is shaped and formed as a follower of Jesus, leadership is compromised and weakened. We are, and must be, spiritual leaders. As such, the way we lead is always in response to our relationship with Jesus: it is the way of the cross, the way of sacrificial love, the way of servanthood, the way of humility, the way of inclusiveness, gentleness, and openness—to others and to God. Our purpose as leaders is not to serve the institution or to maintain the bureaucracy of the denomination; our purpose as leaders is to follow Jesus and invite, encourage, and help others along the way. "As long as we keep purpose in focus in both our organizational and private lives, we are able to wander through the realms of chaos, make decisions about what actions will be consistent with our purpose, and emerge with a discernible pattern or shape to our lives."[9] That shape is and must be cruciform.

LEADERSHIP LESSON TWO

A leader in and for the church sets the direction for the Body and articulates it well. Across the genre of books about leadership, one consistent theme is that leaders have the ability to discern and articulate a vision. Pastoral leaders must continually communicate a vision for the church that then sets the church on a path toward health and vitality within the Kingdom. It is one thing to discern a vision and be absolutely certain that it is a vision from God and in harmony with the gospel; it is quite another thing to communicate it in a way that builds consensus and becomes the driving force within a congregation. As in other conferences and denominations, the Alabama–West Florida Conference has a number of clergy who have caught a vision but neglected to bring the people on board, excite them about the possibilities, and direct them toward the goal. In the twenty-first century, the abilities to communicate, to use every means available to cast a vision, to motivate people, and to chart a course are absolutely essential.

LEADERSHIP LESSON THREE

A leader in and for the church maintains alignment with the vision. Of all the roles that a pastoral leader may be called upon to exercise none may be more important—or more difficult—than guiding the church toward determining what they must stop doing in order to be faithful to the vision. A leader must be able to see the big picture, to determine what is essential in bringing it to reality, and to have the courage to make difficult choices. What we say no to may be one of the most critical choices the church and the denomination make in the coming years. Local churches have a strong tendency to develop routines, rituals, and regulations that started with good intentions but, over time, became hindrances to the vision. Things become ingrained in the system, and eliminating them will result in some people trying to hang on and make life miserable for the leader. Aligning organization, activities, and investments with the vision will require courageous leadership. However, unless the leader stakes out the direction and gets all parts of the system moving toward it, the church (or denomination) will drift and decline.

> The foremost challenge for leaders today . . . is to maintain the clarity to stand confidently in the abundant universe of possibility, no matter how fierce the competition, no matter how stark the necessity to go for the short-term goal, no matter how fearful people are, and no matter how urgently the wolf may appear to howl at the door. It is to have the courage and persistence to distinguish the *downward spiral* from the radiant realm of possibility in the face of any challenge.[10]

LEADERSHIP LESSON FOUR

A leader in and for the church builds community by building up the Body of Christ. A leader in today's environment possesses the keen insight to know that we live in an interconnected, wired, and networked world. The church is, or should be, no different. In fact, if we have been true to our Wesleyan, Methodist roots, we would understand and model connection better than any other organization. A leader understands that no one individual or no one small group or no one church is going to survive very long on its own. That is why a leader must constantly be building and nurturing teams for the work of ministry. It is why a leader must practice collegiality not as a competitor among many others. A leader learns how to build bridges, make connections, and collaborate across the congregation and the world. Jesus used the analogy of the vine and the branches (John 15); Paul used the analogy of the body (1 Cor 12); John Wesley developed a system of a "connexion" all to teach us that community is critical to fruit-bearing ministry in this world. "Servant leadership is not pandering to codependent consumers who want a god to suit their agendas; rather, it is serving those in need in order to reproduce new disciples who in turn will join God's mission."[11]

LEADERSHIP LESSON FIVE

A leader in and for the church maintains stability in the midst of chaos. Managing transitions within the church or denomination, engaging conflict well, maintaining hope and calmness, and being a nonanxious presence are all essential qualities for a leader. In the midst of constant change and turmoil that surrounds life in this time, it is imperative that a leader should keep a healthy balance, a steady hand, and a calm disposition in the midst of chaos. In the absence of this kind of stable leadership, people will gravitate toward anything and anyone promising a way through the mess. While sustaining this kind of calm, nonanxious presence in and for the church, the leader must always point the way toward the kingdom of God with creativity, energy, and passion. It is one thing to be passive and laid-back; it is quite another to be nonanxious and proactive in sorting through the chaos and helping to calm the storm and to lead others through the confusion. There is no place for any sense of resignation or giving up when the chaos is in full gear. That is precisely the time for the pastoral leader to lean on the hope that is ours in Christ Jesus and call people to the light of grace and love.

LEADERSHIP LESSON SIX

A leader in and for the church never stops learning, growing, and going on to perfection. One phrase that has worked its way into the vocabulary of many people and many institutions of higher education is *lifelong learning*. It is the recognition that those who are going to be on the cutting edge of leadership in the coming decades will have to keep learning new things. Technology and the wired world make it possible to study with and sit at the feet of some of the most inspired leaders in the world today. Pastors need to take advantage of every opportunity to learn because, in this information age, knowledge is integral to the success of those being led. Even if seminars or training events are too distant or too expensive, we can take advantage of the wide world of information available at the click of a mouse on the Internet. We can take advantage of what continues to be one of the best ways to learn, grow, and expand: reading! In an article written in 2004 for the *Circuit Rider* magazine, I put it this way: "There is no substitute for reading broadly, deeply, and regularly. By exercising the mind, stretching the spirit, and nourishing the soul, we prepare ourselves to provide the spiritual leadership needed in a world desperate for a vital word of hope and direction."[12]

LEADERSHIP LESSON SEVEN

A leader in and for the church listens and pays careful attention to what the people say, and, more important, to what the Spirit is saying to the churches today. In a world filled with the Babel sounds of conflicting voices, in a world saturated with noise, a leader must be able to step back and hear what is being said in the context of our identity and formation as the people of God. A pastoral leader remains in touch with the people by building relationships and listening to the heart-cries that come forth. We must be more willing to listen than to offer quick, easy solutions to complex and confusing issues. But our listening must not be solely to the voices of the people. There is also the voice of God that breaks through in unexpected and surprising ways. Being attentive to the Word that is revealed in Scripture, paying attention to the movement of God's Spirit in the hearts and lives of others as well as of ourselves, and listening carefully to the prompting and nudging of God enables the leader to point the way forward toward a new day and a renewed church.

PREPARING LEADERS FOR THE FUTURE

Some of the qualities and characteristics of an effective leader are the result of the amazing grace-gift of God, bestowed upon a person. As those gifts are recognized, nurtured, and sharpened, a leader emerges. Leadership is both a gift of God and a development of key abilities that are learned and practiced in the course of a lifetime. John Wesley's enumerating various qualities in his "Address to Clergy" cited earlier certainly recognized that some leadership qualities are inherent, whereas others are learned. This leads to one of the new challenges for the denomination as we move forward. Seminaries must renew their commitment to preparing people and forming leaders to serve as pastors of local churches. To learn and, in some ways, to master the classic theological education curriculum is important: pastors need to know church history, think theologically, sort through the ethical dilemmas this twenty-first-century world faces, and gain skills in exegesis and serious biblical study. But the seminaries must also rededicate their efforts toward preparing men and women to use this knowledge in the service of God *through the local church*. Equipping and preparing pastoral leaders for the church must become the priority. Our several seminaries and national credentialing groups must be intentional in listening not only to the academic guild but also to the church, the bishops, conference leaders, and local church leaders and then in shaping a seminary experience that combines the best of scholarship with the vision of a stronger, more faithful church in this amazing and interesting period of history.

> Pastors need "an entrepreneurial spirit. Plants and turnarounds are not for traditional people. One must be willing to take risks and criticism with humility." (Rural Ausley, Niceville United Methodist Church, Niceville, Florida)

In addition, local churches, district committees,

and conference boards of ordained ministry must recognize their key roles in calling forth the next generation of leaders for the church. Developing a cadre of mentors who are faithful and successful pastors of growing, healthy churches should be a primary task of the conference. In the Alabama–West Florida Conference, the board of ordained ministry and the cabinet have developed a group of coaches who will serve as guides for new seminary graduates, who will walk with them through the period of probation and first appointments, and who will coach them to nurture the gift of leadership for the glory of God and the building up of the Body of Christ. In other words, all of those responsible for developing clergy leaders have a critical role to play in the process. The next generation of clergy leaders must be inspired and called by God, connected and linked to one another, as well as serving and preparing others to serve. It is not an assignment for the fainthearted. Nothing less than those called and gifted by God, and sent by the church to lead, will begin to reverse the downward spiral of Methodism.

CHAPTER FOUR

CORE COMPETENCIES FOR CHURCH LEADERSHIP

In the Alabama–West Florida Conference, the district superin-tendents, the board of ordained ministry, the board of laity, and I have been engaged in conversations focused on what is essential for clergy excellence. We have developed a list of core competencies, which we believe every clergyperson should exhibit in her or his leadership within a local church. There are five: centering, proclaiming, leading, equipping, and engaging. Within these broad categories, certain practices, skills, and abilities further define and illuminate the meaning of each. This way of identifying expectations for clergy excellence allows us to develop evaluation instruments that measure performance and point clergy toward areas that need improvement and strengthening. As this model has emerged we have spent considerable time communicating with laypeople and clergy across the conference. At every opportunity, we have lifted up one or more of the characteristics we have identified and invited feedback. Primarily, we have issued challenges for clergy to pay attention, to develop skills, to enter into evaluation prayerfully, and to take risks by stepping out, learning, and enhancing their abilities. However, the most vital piece of this model is that every person, and most particularly the clergy who are called upon to proclaim, equip, lead, and engage the people of God must be *centered in Christ.*

CENTERING

It is expected that every pastor is growing deeper in her or his relationship with God through Christ Jesus. Although this growth cannot be measured, the fruit of its existence will be visible for all. A minimal expectation is that every pastor should set aside specific times each day for prayer, Bible reading, devotion, meditation, and spiritual formation. This discipline is absolutely essential for enhancing one's leadership and ministry skills, for a deep relationship with God that grows and glows in everyday living, and for preparing one's soul and life for the hard battles that will be encountered. What is at stake here is nothing less than the soul of the clergyperson and the mission of the church—*not* one's career! I suspect that the lay and clergy members of this particular area where I currently serve have grown weary of hearing me say "you cannot give away what you do not have." Even if a church benefits from quality leadership, if there is no depth, no richness, no foundation, no deep well of holiness and spirituality out of which a clergyperson leads, there will be no fruit. The foundation for spiritual leadership in the church is a quality personal relationship with God in Christ that continues to grow and develop. It is this relationship and this form of spiritual leadership that distinguishes us. It is this spiritual dimension that will rescue us from merely becoming another organization or institution focused on the economic bottom line or struggling to survive for a few more years. Leadership in the church is and must be sacred (holy before God) and spiritual before it is anything else. Only as we are centered in Christ will the mind and heart of Christ be revealed in our leadership and lived out through *ecclesia*.

When we ponder what it means to be centered in Christ, we are invited into a spiritual exercise that includes at the very least prayer, scripture, and an intentional focus on the One who calls us, the One who, in the words of Dietrich Bonhoeffer, calls us "to abandon the attachments of this world" and bids us "come and die."[1] We are called to die to self, die to vain dreams of higher

> **"Pastors who are in it for the long haul will build the church they dream of instead of marking time until they get to go to the church they dream of. They develop long-term vision and strategies for the future. When congregations buy into that vision, the church becomes purposeful and powerful."** (Doug Pennington, Lynn Haven United Methodist Church, Lynn Haven, Florida)

steeples and salaries, die to the notion that it is all about *me*. Am I growing, maturing, and deepening in this relationship, or has it stagnated and started to wither? Have I experienced God's mercy that is forgiveness and God's grace that is embodied in a different way of walking, a different attitude and perspective, and a different behavior? Will the mind of Christ be within us and among us? Will we seek first God's kingdom? Is Christ at the center of our living and being? Are we going on to perfection? Is there a balance in our lives and in our ministries between personal and social holiness? Will we order our lives after the example of Christ? Are we doing so more faithfully today, this month than we were last year or a decade ago? To paraphrase Charles Wesley, will we rise, go forth, and follow Jesus?[2]

Each person may choose to participate in a number of disciplines in order to practice holiness and grow more centered in Christ. There are multiple possibilities for retreat, accountability groups, or discipleship and covenant communities. With John Wesley, we ask annually through consultations and conversations with clergy across the Alabama–West Florida Conference, how is it with your soul? It is not a matter of dictating how or in what way one gets centered in Christ, only that we encourage every clergyperson to be deeply rooted in Christ in order to more faithfully fulfill the role and the expectations of ministry in the twenty-first century.

In the mid-1990s, I began an annual pilgrimage to the Abbey of Gethsemani in Kentucky for a retreat of silence and prayer. This is the abbey that was home to Thomas Merton, author of many books and articles on the spiritual life and contemplative prayer. The hospitality of the monks and that annual week of living in silence (or as close to it as we may get in this world) have become a time of spiritual renewal and refreshment for me. Living according to the Rule of St. Benedict, going into the church seven times daily for prayer, chanting the psalms, singing hymns, and reading Scripture provide the structure for each day. The rest of the time is devoted to reading and reflecting, hiking and meditating, and opening my spirit to the impress of God's Spirit. It is a kind of annual rebirth in and refreshment for my soul. It is getting reconnected with the God who is revealed and made known to us in Christ and through creation. It is a time to get refocused on the things of God for my life and for the work of ministry. Although not everyone would find this type of experience beneficial or possible, every clergyperson must find some means, some method, and some rhythm of spiritual renewal. We desperately need this for the culture and society into which we are sent is so filled with noise and so preoccupied with the consumer mind-set that our attention is too often diverted from the things of God, and our lives get off center. During a recent retreat at the abbey I spent time with one of the more recent publications of Thomas Merton. Published long after he wrote it, and long after his death, *The Inner Experience* stated this expectation of being centered in Christ clearly: "The purpose of our life is to bring all our strivings and desires into the sanctuary of the inner self and place them under the command of an inner and God-inspired consciousness. This is the work of grace."[3]

Building from a strong center and grounded in Christ Jesus, excellent, effective ministry for this present time can be identified around the other key roles and responsibilities of the clergyperson. Let me be very clear, repetitive, and overstate the case: unless one is centered in Christ and is nurturing and growing in that relationship, the remaining competencies become mere job descriptions and standards of behavior for a career rather than grace-signs of effective leadership for our vocation of loving and serving God. The inner, spiritual competency is the foundation upon which the other competencies rest. There is a direct correlation between the growth that has been sustained in the Alabama–West Florida Conference and the leadership of the clergy in proclaiming, leading, equipping, and engaging. Each of the remaining competencies is accompanied by two lists of skill sets that can be measured and evaluated so that the clergyperson can be held accountable and can develop a plan for improving and strengthening those skills. One set we call *ministry skills*, those that can be taught, learned, and developed. The other, the *interpersonal skills*, has more to do with relational issues, the gifts with which a person is endowed by God. Each competency and accompanying skill set become a large part of the evaluation instrument that has been developed to reinforce and gauge effectiveness.

PROCLAIMING

"But how are they to call on one in whom they have not believed? And how are they to believe in one in whom they have never heard? And how are they to hear without someone to proclaim him?" (Rom 10:14). This series of questions posed by the apostle Paul goes to the heart of one of the most visible aspects in the life and ministry of a clergyperson. As noted in the last chapter, we are living in an information age, in which news events are beamed almost instantly to all corners of the world. At the same time we are living in an age where the way people receive and retain information, the way people hear and respond is radically different than in previous generations. The multiplication of information-sharing venues generates more opportunities and more challenges for those called to proclaim the good news of Jesus in this world. Paul rightly understood the central importance of the proclamation of Jesus, something that is also

"While I feel that an important lesson is for the elders of our church to go the second mile with compassion, inclusive love, and genuine care for people, I think the one lesson that I would offer to the denomination is for our church to renew an emphasis upon preaching. Though every aspect of ministry is vitally important, I believe the greatest impact a pastor makes upon a congregation and community is through the preaching ministry on Sunday. Quality and spirit-filled preaching draws people to churches, and their lives are changed." (George Mathison, Auburn United Methodist Church, Auburn, Alabama)

emphasized in almost every chapter of the book of Acts. As but one example, Luke records in Acts 16 that as Paul is called to Macedonia, he was "convinced that God had called us to *proclaim* the good news to them" (Acts 16:10, emphasis mine). Later, in Philippi, his accusers announce that Paul and his companions are "slaves of the Most High God, who *proclaim* to you a way of salvation" (Acts 16:17, emphasis mine).

How, then, shall we proclaim in the twenty-first century? In this amazing period of history, as the means of communication continue to expand, those of us in the church cannot rely on outdated methods. We must find new, creative ways of proclaiming the faith. We must connect with people of all ages and cultures in order for them to hear and respond to God's gracious invitation. As we are inundated with information, with a variety of philosophies and perspectives about life, and with a seemingly never-ending flow of disastrous events around the world, the need for good news to be proclaimed is of utmost urgency. That is why the ministry of preaching and teaching must be central to our life and work as pastors called by God and sent by the church. In almost every consultation I have had with laypeople, committees, and members of local churches, the burning plea is for quality preaching. Given the current reality in which we live and given the cry of the church, the need for effective proclamation rises to the top of the list of characteristics for excellent pastors who will lead the renewal of this denomination.

If we are to reverse the decline and turn the denomination around, we must be courageous and bold in our proclamation. This is not a time for timidity. This is not a time for taking the easy path of least resistance, thus maintaining the status quo. This is not a time for compromising our witness. This is not a time for taking the convenient, popular road. Now is the time for seizing the initiative and for showing the way to and through life by boldly proclaiming the gospel of Christ. We are well aware of the way in which the world tries to squeeze us into its mold. This present time demands courageous clergy leaders who are committed to proclaiming Christ Jesus and no other. From our own heritage, John Wesley might indeed be calling us to rediscover "real Christianity" and to spread scriptural holiness across the land. Such a movement could be launched from the pulpits and classrooms of the thousands of churches that are still active in this land. For many, such a movement will require extensive refresher courses in proclaiming and teaching the good news. "In the presence of God and of Christ Jesus . . . I solemnly urge you: proclaim the message; be persistent whether the time is favorable or unfavorable; convince, rebuke, and encourage, with the utmost patience in teaching" (2 Tim 4:1-2).

There are numerous books and seminars available to assist in the strengthening of this skill for ministry. There are theories in abundance: preaching with or without notes, preaching with or without video/DVD/multimedia support, preaching from manuscript or outline, preaching a series of sermons or from the lectionary. What is essential is, as the apostle Paul wrote, proclaiming Christ Jesus. Whatever method or style one settles on as a natural fit for the gifts God has bestowed, the message of the proclamation must be centered on Jesus, and "no other" as the United Methodist ordination vows phrase it. We can possess some essential gifts as excellent communicators, but unless the content of the message revolves around Jesus, we will have missed our opportunity to witness to the one who is hope and salvation for a hurting world. Every proclamation, every moment of teaching, must include an appeal for a faithful following of Jesus in our daily lives, a living out of the gospel in our actions and attitudes, and a deep commitment to a personal relationship with Jesus. Whatever the theme, the focus, or the season, if we fail to proclaim him, we have failed to be faithful to the high calling in Christ Jesus. In an information-saturated world, the good news of Jesus the Christ offers a way through and a hope that transcends divisions, boundaries, and suspicions.

Proclaiming: The Ministry of Preaching and Teaching

Ministry skills (Knowledge)	*Interpersonal skills* (Grace-gifts)
Effective communication	Passion and flexibility
Verbal and nonverbal skills	Connecting with the context
Relating to real-life issues	Creativity and energy
Preparation and organization	Sense of urgency and concern
Evidence of biblical study	Enthusiasm
Prophetic and pastoral skills	Contagious personality

LEADING

The shelves of bookstores and libraries are filled to overflowing with books on leadership. But in determining the kind of leadership required for clergy leading the people of God in ministry and service in the world today, we must be prayerful and attentive to choose paths, ideals, and lists that are in harmony with the gospel. We are called by God's grace to model transformational leadership: transforming lives, transforming churches, transforming communities, and transforming our world. Leading is both a gift and a skill that is extremely important for the life and health of a local congregation.

On behalf of the people of God and to lead the church in fulfilling its mission in the world, clergy are sent to order the life and witness of the church. *Order* is another ordination word and is not to be exercised as command and control, or boss and dictator. In twenty-first-century vocabulary, we must think in terms of *administration* and *alignment*. In the words of the first century in the First Letter of Peter: "I exhort the elders among you to tend the flock of God that is in your charge, exercising the oversight, not under compulsion but willingly, as God would have you do it—not for sordid gain but eagerly" (1 Pet 5:1-2). The word used in this passage is central: *tending*. We are not called or sent to serve as autocratic leaders, exercising unilateral authority over the life of the people or the church entrusted to our care. Tending has a different quality to it. It is about holding the office with care and by grace. It is about leading the people with passion and compassion. It is about recognizing dangers along the way and pointing in a new direction. To lead the church is a grand calling and an immanently significant role. Skills can be taught and practiced and refined. The spirit in which it is exercised is critical. On the shore of the Sea of Galilee one morning, the risen Jesus instructed Peter: "Tend my sheep" (John 21:16). This is still good advice for twenty-first-century leaders.

Leading: The Ministry of Administration

Ministry Skills (Knowledge)	*Interpersonal Skills* (Grace-gifts)
Team building	Objectivity
Problem solving	Efficiency
Conflict transformation	Punctuality ("shows up on time")
Ability to articulate a vision	Accessibility
Motivating people to catch a vision	Knowledge
Time management	
Anticipating the future	

EQUIPPING

In the early years of my ministry and in the aftermath of my graduation from seminary in 1973, the buzzword that occupied our attention was *enabling*. It was—and is—a dangerous word, for it promotes dependence, even codependence, and perpetuates a clergy-dominated church system. We much prefer the concept of *equipping* for this time. It is certainly a biblical concept. All of the gifts of God listed in the fourth chapter of Ephesians are to be employed for one purpose: "to equip the saints for the work of ministry, for building up the body of Christ" (Eph 4:12). This competency is all about the ministry of nurture and care. Perhaps at no other place in this list of core competencies does the concept of partnership and teamwork surface as it does in our intentional use of the word *equipping*. It is at this point that we recognize that we, as individuals—clergy or laypeople—cannot accomplish the mission or carry on the ministry on our own. We must find ways to establish networks and find creative relationships that allow each person, each believer, to use the gifts God has granted.

There may be no greater challenge for clergy in the twenty-first century than to effectively equip others for the work of ministry, recognizing and acknowledging the gifts and talents of others. We are called to bring out the best in others and to help nurture the gifts so that the best multiplies in service to God. Once the gifts and talents are made visible, the clergy must then coach and enhance those gifts, and be willing to delegate and share responsibility with others. It is not enough to suggest that every member is a minister, or that all believers have gifts; there must be training and nurturing and employing gifts for God. "Effective leaders recognize they were not meant to be the doers of all ministry; they know they have a crucial role in inviting, equipping, and releasing others to contribute meaningful service as well. Kingdom impact is multiplied exponentially through leaders who are successful team builders."[4] The ability to care for people, to recognize their gifts, and to help develop those gifts is severely compromised if the clergyperson is unable to get along with people, is confrontational, or lacks the ability to care with the grace of God. In his sermon, "Awake, Thou That Sleepest," Charles Wesley says, "Dost thou know what religion is? That it is a participation of the divine nature: the life of God in the soul of man; Christ formed in the heart."[5]

Equipping: The Ministry of Nurture and Care

Ministry skills (Knowledge)	*Interpersonal skills* (Grace-gifts)
Recognizing gifts and talents in others	Patience
Coaching and enhancing gifts in others	Understanding / Sensitivity
Delegating and sharing responsibility	Kindness / Gentleness
Visitation (hospitals, nursing homes)	Pastoral skill
Counseling and crisis intervention	Confidentiality

ENGAGING

From John Wesley and the origins of Methodism, we learn that we must have both an inward and outward focus. When a church turns in upon itself, it is on a fast track toward extinction. When all the resources of a church are expended to keep the doors open, it is headed for disaster. We believe it is vitally important for clergy to be held accountable for the ways in which she or he leads a church to engage the world, the community in which the building is located, and the people for whom Christ died. The Scriptures are consistent in this emphasis. The themes listed in Isaiah 61:1-2, and quoted by Jesus in his home synagogue (Luke 4:18-19) cannot be done solely inside a church building. Matthew 25 is quite specific about the kinds of activities that are to consume the time, energy, and resources of a disciple. The fact is a church must have an outward focus, and it must engage the world where hurting people are trying to make it one day at a time.

The skills needed to effectively engage the world and its people focus on specific areas of outreach and witness. If the pastor and the church are to be faithful in engaging the world, then every person and every situation must see, hear, and experience the hope of the gospel and the love of God. It will not always be easy; it will be messy; it will anger some; it will inspire others; it will be a key to the growth of the church. It will require courage and compassion within the clergy leader, but we can do nothing less. The mandate of Jesus is clear!

Engaging: The Ministry of Outreach and Witness

Ministry skills (Knowledge)	*Interpersonal Skills* (Grace-gifts)
Evangelism and witness	Courage
Mission involvement	Withholding of judgment
Outreach to all people	Prophecy and compassion
Representing church in community	Hope

CRITICAL CHOICES FOR THE FUTURE

Every annual conference within The United Methodist Church, every judicatory leader within other denominations, and every nonaligned independent congregation understands that the critical factor for the health, growth, and vitality of a local church is clergy leadership! In the Alabama–West Florida Conference, we have simply tried to identify, briefly and succinctly, what is necessary for a pastor to move toward effectiveness and toward bearing fruit within the Wesleyan heritage. Across the area there are a large number of clergy who actually get it, who are growing and serving effectively, and who are willing to take risks to lead churches in new directions. In addition they are willing to invest themselves in sharpening their abilities and learning new skills, to devote themselves completely where they are sent, and to focus their energy and passion on the mission, not on their next appointment or climbing some imaginary corporate ladder. They are deeply committed to grow and bear fruit where they have been planted. There are at least three critical factors that must be addressed by annual conferences in order to encourage, support, and expand this commitment to excellence.

1. ACCOUNTABILITY AND EVALUATION

As mentioned in an earlier chapter, any system, any institution will place a priority on and will value those things that are counted and measured. As we move deeper into the twenty-first century, it will become even more critical for those in leadership positions to reclaim the Wesleyan emphasis for holding one another accountable. Within The United Methodist Church system, much energy has been expended in recent years around the question of the continued viability of the guaranteed-appointment system for clergy, regardless of whether there is evidence of a pastor's ability to make disciples or grow a church. Many voices are suggesting that it has outlived its usefulness, and that it is the reason for poor to mediocre clergy leadership. It is time to shift the conversation from guaranteed appointment to guaranteed accountability. In the Alabama–West Florida Conference, we know that as we hold up the expectations and clarify the performance standards for clergy, accountability must increase. There are certain measurable results that can be reviewed in order to help clergy, congregations, and cabinets determine effectiveness and continuing availability for appointment. There are consequences for failing to lead the church in its evangelistic efforts and in its mission outreach. There are consequences for failing to develop new leaders, failing to model and encourage faithful biblical stewardship, and failing to teach and preach the gospel with prophetic boldness and pastoral compassion. Those consequences may include an appointment to a smaller work with less salary, a career assessment of gifts and grace that may lead to a new place of service or vocation outside the church, or intentional decisions and actions leading to a clergyperson being placed on "location" (United Methodist terminology) that removes the person from active ministry as an appointed pastor.

The denomination must make decisions that will certainly preserve the integrity of fair process but that will also provide for a less encumbered method of holding clergy accountable and removing ineffective clergy. Bishops and cabinets must be willing to take the often difficult and painful step of intervention where no fruit is evident. Such steps are not easy, nor are they popular, but we must ask ourselves what is of primary importance: a kept and protected career clergyperson or the mission of the church.

As a critical piece of accountability, we have developed and implemented a performance review process that attempts to measure the effectiveness of a pastor and to identify those areas where skill enhancement is called for. We are designing our own evaluation instrument that will assist clergy to hold meaningful dialogue with lay leaders of the church in determining strengths and areas where growth is needed. The performance review is built around the four core competencies with both a numeric scale and a narrative space to indicate how well a pastor is achieving the expectations of the church, as well as his or her own hopes and dreams. We have moved the time for the evaluation to take place to the late summer in keeping with the start of a new appointment year, in our United Methodist way of marking out the calendar. This keeps the evaluation away from that period of time when compensation dominates the conversation and away from the time when churches are discerning whether there should be a change of pastoral leadership. All of the raw data and material is forwarded to the district superintendent, who also consults with the clergyperson, reflects on the results, and assists in designing a plan for continuing education and formation.

The key to this process is openness and honesty. We have discovered that many laypeople in local churches are unwilling to offer helpful and constructive feedback, or (at the other extreme) are brutally and unfairly critical of the pastor. We continue to schedule training sessions to equip pastor-parish relations committees in this extremely important task. Not surprisingly, we have also discovered that many clergy are not willing to receive suggestions and recommendations in a spirit of growing toward perfection. They become defensive, argumentative, and angry that anyone would suggest that they need to improve one or more skills. One hallmark of an effective leader is the willingness and the ability to receive feedback and act upon it. If we are going to develop effective, excellent clergy leaders for the challenges of the twenty-first century, then all of us must recognize that we are not perfect and that we must constantly seek to improve and enhance the gifts God has bestowed upon each one. Bishops, cabinets, conferences, and other boards and agencies will have to develop the training events that will address the critical needs for our pastors. In addition, churches will have to be willing to provide the time and resources for clergy to receive the training. Churches must see this as an investment in the future not only for their congregation, but also for the future growth and health of the denomination as a whole.

2. APPOINTMENT-MAKING AND ITINERACY

Based on performance reviews, assessments by district superintendents, consultation with appropriate committees, and prayerful discernment, clergy are sent to serve Christ and the church in a particular community. This is our United Methodist system of clergy deployment, known as itineracy,[6] where the bishop and the district superintendents appoint pastors to the churches across the conference. Itineracy is a strategy for mission in the world. In the tradition of Jesus and the disciples, it is about being called and about following and about being sent. It is about never being content or settled or satisfied with where one is or with what one is doing. Although it has often been highly criticized and ridiculed, and there are certainly flaws in the system, there is enough flexibility built in to allow for the appointment of the right leaders to the right churches, matching gifted pastors with the needs of a particular church and community. What is crucial is that appointments are made based on effectiveness, need of the local church, gifts and skills of the pastor, and the spirit of discernment. Consistently poor performance reviews, a failure to bear fruit, and an unwillingness to improve or strengthen one's skills will result in appointments that may not be up or more demanding. It is one leverage point bishops have.

In the Alabama–West Florida Conference, one of the intentional decisions about clergy leadership has been to encourage and promote longer tenure for pastors in an appointment. In fact, the average length of an appointment of a pastor in this conference, particularly in the growing churches, is almost double the national average. We have learned, often the hard way, that where there is a match of gifts and needs, where the Spirit of God is moving through the pastor and the church, and where effective ministry is happening, there is no need to change pastoral leadership simply for the sake of change. Some of the largest membership churches—and, in most cases, fastest growing churches—across this conference are being led by pastors who have been under appointment to those churches more than fifteen years. This is uncommon across our denomination and puts its own kind of stress and strain on the itinerant system. However, if the ultimate goal is to reach people with the life-transforming, grace-empowering, love-abiding Spirit of God, then we must be willing to invest leadership in those congregations with a long-term vision. We have made the conscious decision (not at all a popular one) to make a significant shift in making appointments: from salary and seniority (the old method ensured that pastors would advance in the system regardless) to faithfulness and fruit. We can no longer be satisfied with the mediocre or the status quo. It is time—it is past time—for clergy to be sent based on abilities, passion, and effectiveness rather than hanging around or hanging on and being taken care of by the old system.

3. LIFELONG COVENANT OF LEARNING

If there is anything that should be apparent to anyone, it is that this world grows more complex and confusing, more chaotic and uncertain, with each passing month. The rapid change that is taking place challenges all of us to shift into a mode of constant learning and growing. For those of us who stand in the Wesleyan tradition, this is nothing new, for we are invited, encouraged, and urged to *go on toward perfection*. Such going on implies movement and growth and new insights and fresh experiences of God's Spirit moving in us and preparing us to serve the present age. Again, Robert Quinn strikes the right note: "One key to successful leadership is continuous personal change . . . a reflection of our inner growth and empowerment. . . . Personal change is the way to avoid slow death."[7]

This means that we must take seriously and enforce the requirement for earning continuing education units. More than simply earning credits, the focus should not be for the sake of fulfilling a requirement, but for the necessity of learning and growing in our ability to serve Jesus with excellence in this present age. If any clergyperson serving in this first decade of the twenty-first century completed all educational requirements for ordination or licensing prior to 1995, it is past time to retool in order to meet the demands and challenges of a new era. About every five to eight years, we must discover new ways to proclaim the gospel more effectively and influence the world with hope and healing in the name of Jesus. The denomination as a whole must decide to invest heavily in preparing persons to serve as clergy leaders, *and* in renewing those same clergy leaders on a regular basis. As noted in the previous chapter, seminaries must decide that the first and most basic reason for existence is to prepare persons to serve God in the world through the church. Boards of ordained ministry must hold every clergyperson accountable for constantly learning and growing in skills and abilities. Clergy can no longer afford the luxurious idea that what was learned at one point in life will suffice for all time.

Developing quality, effective clergy leaders is an essential first step in any process that will reverse the downward spiral of United Methodism in America. This will require cooperation and collaboration on the part of everyone concerned about the future and clergy leaders: local churches from which persons are called, conference boards for credentialing, seminaries for training and equipping, and, bishops and district superintendents for deployment. Unfortunately, across Methodism nearly all those who are preparing for service as pastors of local churches come out of churches that are in decline or have been in decline for decades. The number of clergy who have any image of what it means to grow a church, or to lead a church toward health is small. We perpetuate a system of decline because we have too few models from which passionate, gifted, excellent leaders emerge. Within the Alabama–West Florida Conference, the system is inverted, with the majority of the students enrolled in seminaries coming from healthy, growing churches or dynamic college ministries. They have models and mentors who understand what is needed to make disciples, grow a church, and reach out to new generations of people. What does a thriving, vital, dynamic church look like?

CHAPTER FIVE

VITAL SIGNS OF DYNAMIC CONGREGATIONS

The announcement that Christendom has ended is generally met with skepticism (from institutional employees whose career was based on Christendom) or with denial (from those who, with head in sand, refused to see) or with fear (from those who wonder what will happen next). The reality is that the institutional church as it existed and survived for centuries is in trouble. Movements, programs, and analyses designed to save the church have proliferated to the point where church leaders are lost in an avalanche of words and five-year plans. The Alban Institute promoted a series on "the once and future church," with dreams and plans for revitalizing the church. The "church growth movement" promised a scientific approach to homogeneous growth. The "total quality movement" paralleled the business world with the concept that if we imposed quality and great customer service, the people would return. Other movements such as "seeker sensitive" or "organic" or, now, "emergent" churches serve as metaphors to address the reality of what it means to be a church in a post-Christendom era. All of this analysis and work is addressed primarily to the Western world. As Philip Jenkins has well documented:

> Over the past century . . . the center of gravity in the Christian world has shifted inexorably southward, to Africa, Asia, and

Latin America. Already today, the largest Christian communities on the planet are to be found in Africa and Latin America. . . . Whatever Europeans or North Americans may believe, Christianity is doing very well indeed in the global South—not just surviving but expanding.[1]

Where, then, does this leave those of us who are struggling to hold on and spinning our collective wheels arguing over facts and implications? Whereas Christianity is spreading rapidly in parts of Latin America and Africa, at least two-thirds of the congregations in the United States of all denominations are languishing on life-support. Some pundits place the figure as high as 80 percent. Although every denomination can point with a mixture of pride and relief to a handful of congregations that are doing very well, the reality is that those churches are the exception rather than the rule. The United Methodist Church has its own set of similar disappointing numbers with declines happening in every region of the country, even in places where population growth has exploded. For instance, in the last four decades of the twentieth century, the population of the state of California grew by 116 percent as membership in The United Methodist Church declined by 42 percent. The state of Ohio grew by a modest 17 percent during that time period, but The United Methodist Church lost 39 percent of its membership. Even in the state of Florida, where membership in the church grew by 40 percent (portions of two annual conferences), the actual population growth was in excess of 200 percent. Statistics such as these tell only part of the story; not only are churches declining in numbers, most have become dysfunctional and unhealthy gatherings of aging, like-minded people.

The Alabama–West Florida Conference comprises the lower half of the state of Alabama and the panhandle of the state of Florida, the slowest growth area in the state. Even though the conference membership grew by nearly 20 percent, we did not keep pace with population. Thus, there is joy that unlike much of the rest of the denomination the conference actually showed steady growth but also disappointment that, like the rest of the denomination, we did not keep up with the actual growth of population. The Alabama–West Florida Conference is fortunate to have a number of congregations that worship more than one thousand on any given Sunday, with five congregations worshiping more than two thousand. It is the home conference for Frazer Memorial United Methodist Church in Montgomery, at one time the fastest growing church in the denomination. Frazer has maintained its growth with more than eighty-five hundred members although it is not getting the publicity it received in the 1990s. The conference also has a large number of churches that have an average worship attendance in excess of 350. But, like the rest of the denomination, there are many churches either holding their own or declining or simply trying to keep the doors open for one more year.

> "Encourage each local church to create a mission statement focused upon the Great Commission with specific goals that meet the needs of people in their community . . . create churches with greater compassion for evangelism and dependence upon prayer. Spiritual growth and vibrant, life-changing worship would become an essential part of reaching others for Christ." (Cory Smith, Woodland United Methodist Church, Montgomery, Alabama)

The story of how the Alabama–West Florida Conference has shown a net growth of members of almost 20 percent in the last three decades is not dramatic. There were no magic programs. There were no dynamic explosions of growth in migrating population to account for shifting membership rolls. In fact, as noted earlier, the Alabama–West Florida Conference has no major metropolitan area and none of the demographic projections anticipate any major or significant growth in population. Yet the conference continues to grow. Had the rest of The United Methodist Church grown at the same pace as this one particular area, there would now be nearly fifteen million members, and countless more opportunities for mission outreach and justice ministries and influential voices shaping the life of many communities.

BEYOND SURVIVAL

Soon after my arrival as bishop of the Alabama–West Florida Conference, I embarked on an extensive meet-and-greet tour of the area. Like other newly assigned bishops, I wanted to get to know the area, the geography, the roads, and the heart of the people with whom I would be sharing ministry. The most frequently asked question during this two-month road trip was "what is your vision for our conference?" I made it clear that I brought no preconceived ideas or vision and that no sudden epiphany had emerged. I listened and asked questions about where the people sensed God moving in their lives, in their churches, in their communities, and in the conference. I focused the conversation on our shared ministry and our future together. I knew that the record of membership growth had been long and steady, and I certainly did not want to break that momentum. Instead, I wanted to build on it and to sustain it going forward. Those early conversations then continued and expanded in various conference level committees and groups.

Leading up to my first session presiding at the annual conference in 2001, a chance encounter and conversation became a catalyst for catching a vision. The conference leadership team had already made a decision to use our time at annual conference to seek God's direction for the conference. I had committed to teaching three Bible studies, using the book of Acts as the foundation for the study. We invited people to read *Who Moved My Cheese?*[2] We planned to show the accompanying video and to break the conference into small groups for discussion and reflection. Leading up to that opening session, I recalled a lunch conversation I had been a part of earlier with several pastors. The server at the restaurant had been a friendly, attentive young woman who engaged in conversation with us almost immediately. On her second trip to our table, she looked at us and asked, "Are you all a bunch of preachers?" (She nailed us!) One of the members of our group asked what gave us away. Her response: "you just look and sound like preachers! What kind are you?" Our response was a simple, "United Methodist," to which she rolled her eyes and groaned. "Do you go to church," I asked. "Oh, yes," she quickly responded. "I tried the Methodist church down the road when I moved here, and the people were nice and everything. But it was dead. They were friendly to everyone but me. So now I go to an *alive* church." (She emphasized the word!) She then went on for some time describing the caring of the people, the excitement in worship, and the help the church gave her and "the folk who have less than me." Alive! The word struck a chord in me.

Building on that conversation and images of life, health, and vitality, our study of the book of Acts, and our reflections at several levels, a vision emerged that became a driving force for the Alabama–West Florida Conference: cultivating dynamic, thriving congregations. The *conference* does not make disciples, but the conference-level leadership (starting with the bishop) can create an atmosphere of expectation that every local church will *thrive* and *make disciples* and *be alive*. What that looks like for each congregation will vary in application but not in the substance of being a healthy, vibrant place where the people come together to be the Body of Christ and to extend the Body of Christ into their particular community and the world. The following chart captures some of the contrasting images for churches.

A healthy church *is*	A healthy church is *not*
Vibrant	Dull
Dynamic	Static
Thriving	Surviving
A community	A club
An organism	An organization
Energetic	An institution
Alive	Dead

Every church has signs and symptoms on both sides of this equation. To be healthy, growing, and vital, more of the qualities and characteristics from the left-hand column must be present and experienced than those in the right-hand column. The bottom line is that to be healthy a church must be growing! In fact, if one ceases to grow and change, death is inevitable. Individual members and the corporate body of believers must be growing spiritually, with a deepening faith, and an expanding outreach in the name of Jesus. At the very least a thriving congregation is a place where God's love and grace are experienced and shared, where people discover their spiritual gifts and use them for the glory of God, and where the real needs of people in the local community and around the world are met. It is an invitation to follow and imitate Jesus in action, attitude, and spirit.

Unfortunately, too many churches have adopted a hunker-down and hang-on mentality. Every time a church says, "we are just the right size," it has chosen death over life. Every time a church believes, "we might get so big that we will not know everyone," it has opted for decline and death. Every time a church says, "we may attract the wrong kind of people," it has chosen death over life. Of course, for many congregations now in decline or barely surviving, that choice was made many years ago. The choice may

> "The focus must be on the local church. The strength of the local churches is the strength (or weakness) of the denomination. The strength of the denomination is not found in the boards and agencies or in the general church. The well-being of the local churches is the key to the denomination. The efforts at all levels of the church should be: how do we strengthen the ministry and mission of the local church?" (Glenn Butler, Saint Luke United Methodist Church, Enterprise, Alabama)

have been made by the elected leaders or by the legitimating leaders. The fate may have been sealed because of a series of ineffective pastors, who were either holding on until retirement or who were constantly dreaming of the greener grass that would be theirs on the next rung up the ladder or who were not equipped to lead with excellence.

A conference is only as strong as the individual churches that make up the connection. A denomination is only as strong as the conferences, areas, and regions that unite around a shared purpose of being and living as disciples of Jesus, the tangible Body of Christ in this world. The image we have been painting is captured in the concept of a *thriving congregation*—one that believes there are still people in the immediate neighborhood who must be invited to experience God's grace, mercy, and love; to follow Jesus daily; and to become part of the Body of Christ. Until every local church catches the vision of life and a passion for incorporating people into a relationship with Christ, the downward spiral of the church will continue. In order to move in this direction, local churches must have the full support and encouragement of the bishop, the superintendents, conference leaders, and the denomination. What would happen if The United Methodist Church focused its energy and resources on developing and cultivating healthy, thriving, vibrant *local* churches that have a global impact? Attention and energy must be turned from maintaining the bureaucracy of the institution, from being satisfied with the status quo, and from reorganizing or shuffling the *Titanic's* deck chairs one more time. Resolutions, petitions, and legislative actions will not change the current decline. Relationships, grace, and loving responses to the emotional, spiritual, and physical needs of people will bring life and restore health.

THRIVING CONGREGATIONS

Once the vision of *cultivating dynamic, thriving congregations* was clarified, we took another step in the process. We are convinced that it is only in and through thriving congregations that persons become new, growing, and serving disciples of Jesus. What, then, are the characteristics of a thriving church? What qualities should be visible and alive or developing in each church that is healthy? We discovered that there are plenty of ideas, lists, and definitions, and there are a number of church assessment tools available. In our continuous study of the book of Acts, prayerful reflection, and ongoing conversations, we identified ten characteristics of thriving congregations. We then divided those ten into four broad categories: (1) Spiritual Foundation, (2) Personal Holiness and Maturing Discipleship, (3) Social Holiness and Serving Disciples, and (4) Organizational Stability.

SPIRITUAL FOUNDATION

1. A passionate spirituality that is Bible-based, Christ-centered, Spirit-led and warm-hearted.
2. An inspiring worship service where people encounter and experience the living God.
3. A clear, compelling, and guiding vision statement.

Before we launch into any activity, any ministry project or mission endeavor, a thriving congregation absolutely must be grounded in its identity as the Body of Christ. We are people of God who are led by the Spirit of God. "The point of the Spirit is to enable those who follow Jesus to take into the world the news that he is Lord, that he has won the victory over the forces of evil, that a new world has opened up, and that we are to help make it happen. Equally, the task of the church can't be attempted without the Spirit. . . . Without God's Spirit, there is nothing we can do that will count for God's Kingdom."[3] This kind of Spirit-based, Spirit-led, in-depth relationship that shapes and informs who we are and what we do can be realized in a number of ways, but none more central than in the act of worship. Worship is not about the place or style or hour at which it is scheduled; it is not about traditional, contemporary, or blended, to use the vocabulary that has invaded and infected our churches. It has everything to do with attitude and spirit and transforming relationships through a vital encounter with the living Christ. To ask what we have to do, or what worship style we need to adopt in order to get more people is the wrong question. It simply plays into the hands of the consumer mentality that shops around until something fits or feels good. Rather, the question must be whether or not people actually experience the living God in our services of worship. Do those who attend have a fresh encounter with the living God and risen Jesus? (In that sense, I contend that all worship must be contemporary and relevant, regardless of music styles used.) Do the people have any sense of the awe and wonder of God during the services? Is there a sense of excitement and urgency? Does the style turn people off and away, or does it invite and stir the heart for a life-changing relationship with Jesus? Are the people motivated to go forth to serve a risen Jesus and offer acts of compassion, service, and assistance to those who are hurting on the outside?

PERSONAL HOLINESS AND MATURING DISCIPLESHIP

4. An intentional plan for equipping and empowering laity for ministry.
5. An atmosphere of hope and hospitality where caring relationships exhibit the love of Christ.
6. A vital small group ministry for educating, nurturing, growing disciples and building relationships.

As Wesleyans, a unique focus of our movement is on holiness. For Wesley, the purpose of the societies, even as early as his days in the Holy Club at Oxford, was to encourage, promote, and model holiness of heart *and* life. Wesley's doctrine of perfection captures this sense of holiness, of sanctification, and of growing in our faith. In his sermon "On Christian Perfection," Wesley has a description of what this means. (Again, quoting Wesley directly means utilizing the masculine terminology that dominated his time.)

> We mean one in whom is the mind which was in Christ, and who so walketh as Christ also walked; a man that hath clean hands and a pure heart, or that is cleansed from all filthiness of flesh and spirit; one in whom is no occasion of stumbling, and who accordingly does not commit sin. . . . We understand one whom God hath sanctified throughout the body, soul, and spirit; one who walketh in the light as he is in the light, in whom is no darkness at all; the blood of Jesus Christ his Son having cleansed him from all sin.[4]

To learn, grow, and mature as disciples of Jesus, to nurture personal holiness requires intentional activities designed to assist every person in their daily living and walking in the light of Christ and with the mind of Christ. This is the inward focus of any thriving congregation and must be geared toward not only developing a relationship but also practicing that relationship each day. Churches must find every possible means of providing quality study opportunities for reflecting and interacting with the Word, for enhancing their faith and discovering where God is moving in their lives and in our world, and for practicing the walk. Without this intentional development of personal holiness in our lives, there can be no effective outreach ministry. There may be good deeds and acts of kindness, but without the power of grace and love to model for all persons the gospel and the light of Christ.

SOCIAL HOLINESS AND SERVING DISCIPLES

7. An evangelism and faith-sharing movement that is needs-oriented and people focused.
8. A compassionate and comprehensive mission program (local and global, financial and personal).

At one level, social holiness was, for Wesley, about coming together in community. The class meetings and societies were intended to be supportive and encouraging communities where believers held each other accountable, watching over one another in love. At another level and, admittedly with more twenty-first-century connotations, social holiness could also be about reaching out to meet the needs of others. Today, we too easily equate social holiness with a social gospel, a political agenda, or an involvement in addressing injustices and inhumanity. Both themes are essential for churches to thrive and flourish today: gathering for accountability and mutual support and scattering for service in the world, gathering for deepening the faith and scattering for living the faith, gathering to experience and receive the means of grace and scattering to practice and share the marks of grace, gathering to engage in acts of piety and scattering to engage in acts of mercy.

One of the most powerful and visible ways for a congregation to discover new life for itself, and to become a vital church, is to give itself away. It is imperative that every church see itself as a mission station in the community and for the world, and that every church offers itself to others in the name of Jesus. "All healthy congregations are missional. . . . True spirituality is being joined to God's mission."[5] And God's mission is focused on extending the Kingdom, inviting persons to join the journey, practicing holistic evangelism, meeting needs, and reaching out to those who are hurting, lonely, forgotten, neglected, or marginalized. A thriving congregation, however, understands that personal holiness *must* precede social holiness, both as the community gathered and scattered. Both are needed, but unless we are clear about our identity and secure in our foundation, our acts of mercy becomes a series of niceties and good deeds.

As disciples of Jesus, we are challenged to be involved in hands-on mission projects, in sharing God's love in tangible ways, and in working together to witness to our faith. John Wesley and the early Methodists were out in the streets among the people we today tend to call the working poor. In activities that sound strangely modern, Wesley was very involved in handing out clothes, providing food, and even starting medical clinics to assist people. In a 1786 sermon, Wesley offers insight into our mission among the sick and the poor. His sermon "On Visiting the Sick" suggests that we begin by inquiring about the outward condition of the people we encounter. We are to ask whether they have the basic necessities of life: food, clothing, and fuel for the cold weather. Wesley refers to these as "little labors of love" that open the door that will take us to matters of even more importance. That is, once we have demonstrated our active concern and *agape* love, and addressed their physical needs, Wesley says, we proceed to talk about the conditions of their souls. This combination of mission outreach and evangelistic concern is an essential mark of a thriving congregation today. Because of this topic's critical importance to the turnaround of this denomination, chapter 6 will be devoted entirely to it.

ORGANIZATIONAL STABILITY

9. A functional structure and organizational system where spiritual gifts are recognized and utilized for the Body.
10. A connectionally committed United Methodist Church through participation and support and extravagant generosity.

The last several General Conferences of The United Methodist Church have taken actions to free churches from an overbearing, repetitive institutional structure. With the exception of a few necessary committees, local churches are left to create a system that works, that maintains accountability, and that ensures that all entities within the church are cared for and directed. Local churches must be intentional in designing a system that makes sense and that takes into account their location and context for mission and ministry. The system must be focused on keeping the vision alive, on aligning the components of the structure with that vision, and on allowing the gifts of the people to surface and be utilized for building up the Body of Christ. Margaret Wheatley has written extensively and with keen insights into the inner workings of systems and organizations. In her book *A Simpler Way*, she helps us think about human organizations.

In every organized human activity, self-organization is occur-
ring all the time. . . . In life, systems create the conditions
for both stability and personal discovery. . . . Stability is
found in freedom—not in conformity and compliance. We
may have thought that our organization's survival was guaranteed by finding the right form and insisting that everyone
fit into it. But sameness is not stability. It is individual freedom that creates stable systems. It is differentness that enables
us to thrive.[6]

Sameness is not the key to stability. Rather, we must focus on
and organize around the core values we share: to be the people of
God, called by God in grace and sent into the world to witness
and serve. We are part of the Wesleyan family known as United
Methodists. The emerging trend among many churches is to
eliminate the denominational label and seek to incorporate people into a community of faith. In this choosy, consumerist society, we dare not hide our Wesleyan theology or our United
Methodist flavor. If this is done so that we can be attractive to
the church-shoppers of today and we try to market ourselves to
the latest trends and interests of the consumer, then we will fail
to live out the call and vision of God's Reign. In the name of
being popular or acceptable, Wesley never backed away from
naming perfect love or from calling people to a life of holiness. It
is hard to imagine holiness while at the same time allowing material possessions to define who we are. To be a thriving United
Methodist congregation, churches must claim our heritage,
organize in ways that are consistent with the values and principles of that heritage, and function in a supporting role in the
incredible expansion of Methodism across the globe.
Unfortunately too many churches spend an exorbitant amount of
time, energy, and resources on preserving the institution without
the first three categories that actually give life to the church.

These ten characteristics have become the basis for evaluating
and holding local churches to high standards of expectation. To
assist in that conversation we have developed a one-page dash-
board of vital statistics to help churches look at their trends over

a six-year period. Churches can begin to identify where their strengths are to build on them, where their challenges are to address them. In essence, we say that to be a thriving congregation, churches must have a strong spiritual foundation, an inward focus toward growth and development of disciple-believers, an outward focus on mission outreach, and a functioning, stabilizing plan of organization. "The church is the single, multiethnic family promised by the creator God to Abraham. It was brought into being through Israel's Messiah, Jesus; it was energized by God's Spirit; and it was called to bring the transformative news of God's rescuing justice to the whole creation."[7]

STRATEGIES FOR THE FUTURE

If United Methodism is to reverse its decline, it will happen in healthy churches, not in an expanding bureaucracy, not in more programs and initiatives that do not connect with the pew or the street, and not in larger budgets and greater financial demands from a top-down pyramid. The general church and its various agencies will not be the source of denominational turnaround. Rather, as we invest in helping local churches come alive, grow, and expand mission outreach, locally and globally, we might yet be a turnaround denomination. Thriving churches are focused on developing an attitude and spirit to reach out to new people, new generations, new immigrants, and new populations. The Alabama–West Florida Conference has, over time, nurtured a mentality that focuses on growth. The number of churches that have broken through the three-hundred-in-worship plateau have become the source of more new disciples and more persons hearing the call of God to serve as elders, deacons, licensed pastors and lay speakers than in churches with fewer than two hundred in worship. Denominational leaders—starting with bishops—will have to lead the way in promoting and encouraging growing churches and stop propping up declining, dying churches that drain resources and distract from the mission.

The book of Acts has become for us a defining study and guiding scriptural reference. The story of the church as it emerges, grows, and engages the world that is told in that book is inspiring, insightful, and full of hope and promise. Reading, studying, and learning from those models, several key strategies emerge. We are convinced that these are critical to our growth and to the future of United Methodism in America.

ACTS 2 CHURCHES—
CONGREGATIONAL TRANSFORMATION

In 2001 we began studying the entire book of Acts, starting with those opening chapters, and the birth of the church in the aftermath of the death, resurrection, and ascension of Jesus. We explored the second chapter of Acts and looked for clues to the incredible outbreak of the church and the movement that was the Jesus Way in the first century. Even as we were involved in this reflection, other bishops also began to talk about Acts 2, and together we have begun to chart a course that uses the language of becoming Acts 2 churches. The episcopal address that I delivered in June of 2006 used the vocabulary of Acts 2 to point toward congregational renewal and revitalization through thriving churches.

The Pentecost story that opens the second chapter of Acts reminds us that a thriving church is *noisy* (the sound like the rush of a mighty wind). A thriving church is *messy* ("tongues of fire" do not leave anything the way it was before). A thriving church *embraces change!* They spoke in other languages (that was new!); they were different people who were willing to live different in order to practice the gospel (that was a radical change)! A thriving church is *inclusive*—men and women, young and old, people of all ethnic, racial, social, and economic backgrounds. Acts 2 closes with a picture of a healthy, thriving church that is bursting on the scene. Peter's Pentecost sermon created quite a stir! Then Luke describes the aftermath:

So those who welcomed his message were baptized, and that day about three thousand persons were added. They devoted themselves to the apostles' teaching and fellowship, to the breaking of bread and the prayers. Awe came upon everyone, because many wonders and signs were being done by the apostles. All who believed were together and had all things in common; they would sell their possessions and goods and distribute the proceeds to all, as any had need. Day by day, as they spent much time together in the temple, they broke bread at home and ate their food with glad and generous hearts, praising God and having the goodwill of all the people. And day by day the Lord added to their number those who were being saved. (Acts 2:41-47)

The first component of an Acts 2 church is the incorporation of new believers into the Body. Imagine, after Peter's sermon, there were three thousand new believers. That is quite a contrast for us today where many United Methodist churches are convinced that one or two new believers a year is pretty good. Imagine, day by day the Lord was adding to their numbers, yet we think in annual terms. If we are not adding new believers to the faith, we are not fulfilling our purpose nor accomplishing our mission. On Pentecost, the whole church became evangelists, rushing into the streets (outside the building) to tell others about Jesus and then incorporate them into *ecclesia*. In the twenty-first century the urgency of telling that same story and offering Christ to a hurting world demands a similar kind of whole church evangelistic, new-believer orientation. Our strategy for turning around local churches and the denomination must be a renewed effort to recover our Wesleyan evangelical heritage and reach persons with the life-saving power of the gospel of God's grace and love, revealed in Jesus Christ. Without this, we will continue to flounder, drift, and gradually die.

The second component of the Acts 2 church was inspiring worship, which was and now must be a central guiding force. Acts 2 tells us that a core feature of the life and identity of the church was worship, breaking bread, prayers, and being together in the temple. As these believers tried on their new life in Christ, worship was where they found the courage to live faithfully. Their worship was inspired and inspiring because they anticipated and responded to God's Spirit that flowed into their midst. The Acts 2 believers faced the subtle and sometimes blatant pressures of a pagan worldview, along with threats of oppression and even death. But in their worshiping community, they found the power to live a radically new life in Christ, and were emboldened to venture forth "like sheep into the midst of wolves" (Matt 10:16).

The third component of an Acts 2 church is its focus on outreach and mission: they shared what they had. They gave away their possessions. They took care of any who had need. They loved one another, and reached out to people that the rest of society overlooked and neglected. A dynamic church is one that not only preaches about mission but also practices it, that not only receives offerings for various projects but also sends people out on mission teams to work and serve among all God's children in all places—at home or across the seas. Such projects and outreach are but the beginning of being a church that is not turned in upon itself, but that is creatively engaged on behalf of justice and mercy and hope in the name of Jesus. When a church decides that its entire budget and energy will be focused on itself, it has missed the point of the gospel. The only way to life and to vitality for a congregation is to imitate the way of God in Christ in outreach to the world.

Finally, an Acts 2 church exhibits signs and wonders. What a description! It is as if Luke is saying, "there are some amazing things going on but I really cannot describe them—you just know it and feel it. And it is awesome!" Signs and wonders are not so much about specific activities as about the spirit in and atmosphere of a church. It is that sense of enthusiasm that Wesley was accused of having, and that today the people called Methodists must recover in order to change the church and change the world into the image of Jesus. How? Where do we start?

Again, the answer can be found in the second chapter of Acts. When Peter's sermon is finished (Acts 2:14-36), those who were listening were "cut to the heart" (Acts 2:37). The crowd wanted to know what to do with their severed, convicted hearts. Peter's answer, in a word, was "repent."[8] If we are going to cultivate and develop Acts 2 churches, all of us, laypeople and clergy, must repent. We will need to repent of our complacency and of our hesitancy to name the name of Jesus boldly. We will have to repent of our contented, smug attitudes that *my* church is like a family and there is no room for nonfamily members. We will have to repent of saying, in effect, we really do not care about the rest of the world outside *our* four walls. We will have to repent of believing that God loves *us* more than others. We will have to repent of our efforts to block the movements of God's Spirit in our midst. And we will have to repent of the misplaced loyalty that says that an ever-expanding, bureaucratic, institutional church will save the denomination. Those are indeed hard words, and even harder choices that local church leaders and denominational leaders will have to make. If we as The United Methodist Church really believe that the local church is the place where disciples are made then the priority of every bishop and every general agency must be centered on cultivating thriving congregations. That was and is our choice in the Alabama–West Florida Conference.

ACTS 2 CHURCHES—CONNECTING AND NETWORKING

No individual church can rest on its past, grow comfortable with where it is, or become complacent with the way it is. Through constant study and serious engagement with the Scriptures in small groups, in large gatherings, in formal and informal ways, members of local churches must be deeply involved in discovering new movements of God's Spirit. Through constant study of the neighborhood and local community, members of local churches must discover fresh approaches to sharing the gospel, living as the Body of Christ, and extending hospitality and reconciliation to all those who are hurting. We know all too well that many churches get stuck in their ways and mistakenly believe that if others would just get with it (the way *we* define it) everything would be well with the world and the church. After all, 1 Corinthians 12 gives us a metaphor of the church as the Body of Christ, an image used throughout this book. It is the place where every part, every person, every gift is celebrated and utilized. It is the place where we practice imitating Christ in our life together and in our ministry. It is, after all, what Jesus said would happen. "The one who believes in me will also do the works that I do and, in fact, will do greater works than these" (John 14:12).

In the Alabama–West Florida Conference we encourage local churches to link together to study communities, people, and Scripture to discover new ways to work together to meet needs and practice the faith—not in the spirit of competition, but in the Spirit of Jesus. District superintendents sometimes initiate these partnerships and sometimes resource them. However, even if the district or conference does not initiate them, nothing prevents local churches from making the first move: permission is granted for the sake of the mission! We have also been intentional about lifting up models of effective ministry and how we can—and must—learn from and with one another. Churches tend to expand their own life and ministry when they are networked with another church that is similar in size or location or community need. Our new definition of connection, based on our wired and networked world is much more localized and particularized. When everyone gets together (as in the annual conference session), we worship and celebrate more than we do the same old report-style business. In 2004 and 2005, for instance, we dispensed with the business sessions of the annual conference for one day and sent all the delegates *out of the pew and into the world* to perform hands-on mission projects in the name of Jesus. In 2007, we interspersed stories of thriving churches with the procedures of the conference in order to celebrate and inspire. Following the sessions, we made all the stories available on DVD to be shown across the conference. Our new networks are extending Wesley's view of conferencing and pushing it closer to the people and members, where it all started in the first place. We are learning together, supporting one another, and networking for mutual growth.

ACTS 2 CHURCHES—PLANTING NEW CHURCHES

We know from the history of the Methodist movement in the United States that the greatest times of growth and expansion came when the denomination was starting churches at the phenomenal rate of at least one each day. The genius and commitment of the system was to go where the people were living and, in many cases, to be there ahead of them. The circuit riders and lay leaders and exhorters combed the trails, the passes, the waterways, and the wilderness with a passion for scriptural holiness and for persons who had not yet experienced God's grace and a redemptive, reconciling relationship with Jesus, the personification of God's love in and for the world.

> **"In order for churches to grow, I believe it is essential that the pastor trust her/his congregation and allow them to do ministry. When a layperson has a passion to do ministry or to implement a new mission, I believe it is best for the pastor to get out of the way and offer guidance only as the need arises. . . . The wise pastor will allow the people time to own a ministry before the pastor initiates it." (Art Luckie, First United Methodist Church, Demopolis, Alabama)**

Today there is a new frontier that does not look like the one of the nineteenth century. The wilderness in which many people in the United States live today is covered with concrete or asphalt. The houses are no longer log cabins with dirt floors but are covered with heavy mortgages and empty rooms. The frontier far too many people confront today is filled with the empty spaces of the inner city, the broken windows, doors, and hearts of a people trapped in desperate living conditions. The faces of prospective members used to be rugged from battling the weather and an untamed landscape. The faces today are void of hope, with blank eyes staring from behind doorways in rundown developments. The landscape is a mix of rich and poor, young and old, and a multitude of ethnic backgrounds; renters in housing projects, owners of upscale loft condominiums, and people who pay no rent or mortgage but who sleep under the overpass. We must rediscover some lessons about going where the people are, like our frontier circuit riders and class leaders.

New churches provide fresh and different opportunities for people to hear the gospel, experience the grace, and commit themselves to follow Jesus. What we have learned, however, is that the twenty-first century requires a radically new way of planting churches, with expectations that are big enough to put faith to the test. Planting new churches does not mean that we give up on the existing churches. It does mean that we are committed to reaching new people, and that we know, regretfully, the majority of existing churches do not reach and include new people. If anything, existing churches, more often than not, exhibit all the characteristics of a closed system, with only a few select individuals allowed entrance. It does not have to be that way. It absolutely should not be that way! There are some congregations that can make the shift to a more open, inclusive, embracing system that welcomes new people—even those who do not look the same or speak the same language. But by far the best way to reach new generations and new demographics is through the planting of new churches. We have made a conscious decision to strategically start new churches across the Alabama–West Florida Conference. These new church starts include nontraditional churches, multicultural and multiracial churches, and inner city churches in addition to suburban ones in population growth areas. We have supported and encouraged multisite locations for existing churches, and we have created partnerships for mutual ministry, leadership, and growth. We have not always been successful, and we have had to halt some church starts for a failure to take root and grow.

If The United Methodist Church is going to reverse its downward spiral, it must reclaim its heritage of starting new churches.

The denomination *must* make the critical choice to implement a national strategy of starting new churches, reaching new people, and generating a new passion for spreading scriptural holiness across this land. Planting 350 new churches annually is not beyond the realm of possibility. If each of the other conferences in the United States simply duplicated the steady pace we have already set in the Alabama–West Florida Conference, the denomination would be 75 percent of the way to that goal. However, if we continue to argue over who, where, and how; if we continue to do battle with one another by in-fighting and turf-protecting over ownership; and if we fail to seize the moment to plant new churches and faith communities across the country, then The United Methodist Church in the United States will continue on its current trajectory. The denomination must make a strategic decision to plant Acts 2 churches that will each grow to more than three hundred in worship within five years. Seminaries will have to gear up leadership and church planting tracks to help equip the next generation of pastors. General agencies will have to eliminate some projects and programs—at least for a period of time—so that resources, energy, and investments can be made in reaching new people, who become new disciples, who engage in justice and mercy ministries with others, who reach new people, and the cycle becomes a continuous loop.

ACTS 2 CHURCHES—FROM EPISODIC TO APOSTOLIC

Far too many churches have allowed a fascination with the world, with culture, with marketing, or with what has worked in the past to strip any sense of identity and purpose. Churches have become so enamored with trying to be relevant or to become a convenient club of like-minded people who enjoy each other's company that "you have abandoned the love you had at first" (Rev 2:4). Nowhere are these observations more apparent than in what fills the calendars and occupies the activities of many of our church buildings. Believing that it must be *doing* something, churches opt for episode after episode to fill time, occupy space, or get people in the doors, regardless of the mission. A steady diet of *episodic* activities does not necessarily shape disciples or form servants to follow Jesus into the world and engage in God's mission in and for the world.

There are plenty of options from which to pick and choose, often based on what the church down the street is doing: Bible studies and courses written by the latest popular sage or guru; classes on parenting, financial freedom, exercise, yoga and diet; twelve-step support groups for every imaginable addiction; picnics, ski trips, and sports teams; and on and on. The *episodes* are designed to keep the church open and to give the appearance of life. There is nothing wrong with most of these episodes and any of them could become an excellent vehicle for outreach. However, if those activities are simply held at the church facility or scheduled to entertain, fill time, or give the members something to do, then the church and its leaders have missed the intent of what it is called to be. If those episodes are planned only because someone saw it work in another place, or heard that it was a good thing to do, or believe that it will save the church, then the church itself has become a mere clearing house for chaotic commotion that does not make disciples or shape followers for fruitful witness in the world.

The crucial decision that must be made is for the church (read here denomination, conference, district, and local congregation as a whole) to recover its *apostolic* nature—that is, being sent into the world on a mission. What is needed in this twenty-first century is for the events of the church to be implemented in the name and spirit of Jesus. Questions as simple as "what does this have to do with Jesus?" or "how is this part of the Jesus mission?" may lead to a serious spiritual evaluation of the many activities that fill a church calendar. The focus of the church must be on nurturing, empowering, and equipping persons to be on God's mission to and for a broken humanity. N. T. Wright issues the call for such an *apostolic* church:

> [T]hrough the church God will announce to the wider world
> that he is indeed its wise, loving, and just creator; that through

Jesus he has defeated the powers that corrupt and enslave it; and that by his Spirit he is at work to heal and renew it. The church exists, in other words, for what we sometimes call "mission": to announce to the world that Jesus is Lord. This is the "good news," and when it's announced it transforms people and societies.[9]

Renewing our *apostolic* nature means coming together to pray, study, and support one another; then, having been shaped and formed by the Spirit of God, it means being sent into the world to declare and to live the gospel, starting in the neighborhood or region where a building happens to be located. The United Methodist Church must find the spirit and will to reconnect with and support local churches in their mission in the world. Instead of merely writing that "local churches provide the most significant arena through which disciple-making occurs,"[10] the attention, energy, and resources of the denomination must be turned toward assisting all of us in our common mission. It will not be an easy journey for there will be many activities that will cease in order to recover our passion for the mission and "to equip the saints for the work of ministry, for building up the body of Christ" (Eph 4:12).

CHAPTER SIX

GOING ON TO . . . GREATNESS

In The United Methodist Church today, we have thousands of good churches, filled with millions of *good* people who do countless *good* things and consider themselves *good* church members. The dilemma is that with all this goodness going around, the denomination continues its rapid downward spiral. We still consider ourselves a good denomination, with more members than most other Protestant denominations in the United States. But it is precisely that good assessment that prevents us from making the radical and necessary changes to reverse the trend and become a great denomination, serving an awesome God, whose great grace is extended to people of all nations, races, and generations.

Jim Collins begins his best selling book with six alarming words: "Good is the enemy of great."[1] There may be no better description of the dilemma within The United Methodist Church in America today. In a brief monograph published in 2005, Collins takes the principles and insights from his larger book and applies them to the "social sectors" and "nonprofits." On both the opening and closing pages of that little addendum, Collins writes:

> Mediocre companies rarely display the relentless culture of discipline—disciplined people who engage in disciplined thought

and who take disciplined action—that we find in truly great companies. A culture of discipline is not a principle of business; it is a principle of greatness."[2]

This is perhaps the single most important point in all of *Good to Great*. Greatness is not a function of circumstance. Greatness, it turns out, is largely a matter of conscious choice, and discipline.[3]

Of the hundreds of denominations that exist in America and around the world today, it should be a given that United Methodists understand the role of discipline for our lives, for our churches, and for our denomination. After all, we have a book we call the "Discipline." It turns out, however, that although we may have the title, we do not seem to have a will to discipline ourselves for greatness, to make the choices that will put us on the road to greatness, or to stop doing a myriad of "good" things that end up draining resources, energy, and passion that could be channeled toward greatness. We have not disciplined our thoughts or actions to agree on a mission, vision, purpose, or direction for the future of our church without a substantial amount of quarrelling, arguing, and finally dismissing whatever may emerge from some voice or corner of the denomination. At this point in our history, on this stage of the world's complex agenda, we have a choice. Stay the course and continue the decline, or enter onto the hard road of radical transformation and, by God's grace, grow toward greatness. "Turning good into great takes energy, but the building of momentum adds more energy back into the pool

> **"If we aren't convinced that people need Jesus, we probably won't go to much trouble to help them find him . . . we believe in the power of God to transform."** (Ralph Sigler, Harvest United Methodist Church, Dothan, Alabama)

than it takes out. Conversely, perpetuating mediocrity is an inherently depressing process and drains much more energy out of the pool than it puts back in."[4] We have muddled our way into mediocrity long enough.

Where do we turn to help us make the shift from good to great? How do we find the energy to put an end to mediocrity and to launch into a disciplined new way? We can make this radical turn through a rediscovery of John and Charles Wesley and the evangelical revival that had their fingerprints all over it. Together, they launched a movement, engaged in organizing and giving stability to that movement and proclaimed in word, song, and deed grace that became ingrained in Methodism as prevenient, justifying, and sanctifying. Kenneth J. Collins has studied and written extensively on the Wesleyan movement, and has identified key moments in Wesley's life and emergence as a theologian. Collins points to the May 1738 experience at Aldersgate Street as one defining moment in Wesley's life, one that launched him from that evening prayer meeting into the forefront of the revival in England.

> [S]hortly thereafter, in April 1739, Wesley was determined to continue to *proclaim* the glad tidings of salvation to the middling classes of Britain and, of course, to the poor. By 1741, as the great Evangelical Revival was underway, Wesley took the next step, so to speak, and continued the genius of the Protestant Reformation by conceiving the sheer gratuity of grace not simply in terms of justification and regeneration . . . but in terms of entire sanctification as well. . . . In short, Wesley now connected key Reformation insights, with respect to grace and faith, with the full scope of the holy living tradition he so loved.[5]

The genius of the theological insights of John Wesley in the eighteenth century must become the foundation of what is left of the movement known as United Methodism in America. The key to our future lies in our past. With a renewed application of Wesley's evangelical spirit and with a continual rediscovery of Wesley's theology of perfection and holy living, there is hope for transforming the denomination and radically altering our future. Wesley fervently practiced and urged the people called Methodists to discipline themselves in order to participate in God's mission in the world. Wesley's emphasis on perfect love (both of God and of neighbor), his attention to the needs of poor and the neglected, and his focus on winning souls for Jesus incorporate the best of who we can be as United Methodists today. It is that perspective that motivates churches across the Alabama–West Florida Conference and results in growth.

RECLAIMING JOHN WESLEY

Much has been written comparing the twenty-first-century world with the first-century world. There is a sense in which the proliferation of gods that dominated the first century after the birth, death, and resurrection of Jesus is not unlike our present time. In Acts 17, Paul encounters such a view in his stroll through Athens. Similarly, ours is a time that, although not aggressively hostile toward the Christian faith to the extent that there are persecutions and executions of believers, exhibits benign neglect and indifference toward the Christian movement. It is hard to argue with this line of comparison and there are many who can articulate the connections and similarities in great detail. The church finds itself in very interesting times—having glimpsed God's Reign in the person of Jesus and praying at least weekly for "your kingdom come . . . on earth as it is in heaven" (Matt 6:10) but finding itself in the position of being a small voice on the edge.

There is another line of comparison that may bear more urgently upon us in this time: the relationship and likeness of the church and society of the twenty-first century with the church and society of eighteenth-century England.

> An insular mindset pervaded the consciousness of the developing English nation . . . their developing national identity centered in large part in their monarchy, would eventually

develop a religious establishment that was unabashedly nationalistic, legally centered in the monarchy, and strongly antipapal. The monarchy is the central feature of English history through at least the eighteenth century.[6]

It is not too difficult to recognize the growing endorsement of an American nationalism in many of the churches of this denomination and other Protestant bodies in this country. In one sense of the word, for the people of Wesley's time, the society was culturally Christian, with cathedrals or parish churches in every village and hamlet, yet there were empty pews in every place. Heitzenrater describes something of that culture and setting in which Wesley was shaped and out of which he worked. "Oxford University in the early eighteenth century reflected many of the problems that characterized English society as a whole . . . 'a comfortable slackness' prevailed in the spiritual and academic endeavors of the University, representing a low point in the history of the school."[7]

Indeed, it can be said without too much exaggeration that the American church of the twenty-first century has a certain slackness to our life—good, not great. The church continues to exist, and draw a relatively large number of people, but with little or no enthusiasm and with little or no urgency to practice faithfully the life of a disciple of Jesus outside of Sunday morning. The society as a whole tolerates the faith so long as it does not interfere with the consumer mentality of get, grasp, and hold at all costs. The widening gap between those who have vast financial resources and those who are on subsistence income is a blight upon our society. The growing number of "working poor" is alarming in a country of abundance. The message to accumulate and hoard is seldom challenged by those who proclaim the Jesus who challenged the power structure and religious establishment of his time. Our churches, like those of England in the eighteenth century, have become routine, regular, predictable, and downright boring. Little wonder that fewer and fewer people show up! In a comment on Wesley's "An Earnest Appeal to Men of Reason and Religion," Richard Heitzenrater summarizes our legacy: "Wesley reiterates a familiar base in an opening 'rude sketch' of the doctrine he teaches: Methodism moves beyond a lifeless, formal religion to one worthy of God, and that is love—love of God and love of neighbor, seated in the heart and showing its fruits in virtue and happiness."[8]

The hope for our denomination will be found in reclaiming Wesley's great emphasis on love of God and neighbor, which was the foundation of his bold evangelical spirit. It is time for the people called Methodists in this day to step forth and proclaim with boldness the richness of our evangelical heritage in its Wesleyan context. Here, again, is the challenge to move outside our settled mediocrity in order to rediscover the depth and power of our Wesleyan movement.

> Eighteenth-century Methodism was built upon, and became a contagious worldwide movement because of John Wesley's apostolic vision and message and his vivid sense that a "people of one book" could "reform the nation and spread Scriptural holiness across the land." Often, in the history of denominations, a later generation of leaders will assume they "know better" than their more brilliant founder. . . . Too many of our leaders have flitted from one new theology to another to another. A majority of Methodists are now afflicted with something like amnesia; they have no living memory of what it means to be followers of Jesus Christ in the tradition of Wesley.[9]

It is time to recover from our amnesia and reclaim our Wesleyan evangelical roots, not in an outdated revivalistic mode, but in the richness of Wesley's own doctrine of perfection, knowing that "the only thing that counts is faith working through love" (Gal 5:6). We must reclaim the connection that was so prevalent in the sermons, journals, and other writings of Wesley: both personal holiness and social holiness, both inward religion and outward religion; both evangelism and social action. Far too many voices within Methodist circles today place a greater weight on one side or the other, either on the side of social justice issues or on the side of evangelistic zeal. Either way presents an unbalanced and non-Wesleyan perspective. In one of his late-in-life sermons (from 1789 in fact), Wesley proposed to address "Causes of the Inefficacy of Christianity." His basic question was simply "why has Christianity done so little good in the world."[10] More targeted, Wesley wondered, "why is not the spiritual health of the people called Methodists recovered."[11] He then goes on to detail what has become a familiar dictum for many Wesleyans: gain, save, and give all you can. But therein, according to Wesley, is the heart of the problem: personal and social holiness are not visible in the lives and practices of the Methodists.

> O that God would enable me once more . . . to lift up my voice like a trumpet to those who *gain* and *save* all they can, but do not *give* all they can! . . . See that poor member of Christ, pinched with hunger, shivering with cold, half naked! Meantime you have plenty of this world's goods—of meat, drink, and apparel. In the name of God what are you doing? . . . preferring the fashions of the world to the commands of God? . . . I am determined to be a Bible Christian, not almost, but altogether. Who will meet me on this ground? Join me on this, or not at all.[12]

Wesley's words, coming near the end of his own life and ministry, sound a clarion call to those of us who stand in his legacy, the heritage of inward and outward love, and evangelism and justice ministries in the name of Jesus. Indeed, if we reclaim Wesley we will reclaim the "both-and" nature of holiness; and we will boldly say that without personal holiness there is no social holiness, there is only a nice club doing good things in the world on behalf of humanity. We must also say that without social holiness there is no personal holiness, only an assembly of people dreaming of some vague notion of heavenly escape. However, it must be said that personal holiness precedes social justice activities, for we must have our hearts and souls reconciled, regenerated, justified, and sanctified *before* we venture forth to serve others, love neighbor, and imitate Jesus. It is not to be—it cannot be—reduced to one or the other, but there must be a healthy balance on both sides of holiness.

FOR THE TRANSFORMATION OF THE WORLD

Paragraph 120 of the 2004 edition of *The Book of Discipline of The United Methodist Church* sets the agenda for the denomination: "The mission of the Church is to make disciples of Jesus Christ. Local churches provide the most significant arena through which disciple-making occurs." Since that language was added to the vocabulary of The United Methodist Church, there has been endless debate and sometimes division as we struggle over exactly what it means and how it is to be done. To be theologically correct, we know that *we* do not make disciples. Rather, that is the work of God's grace active in a person's heart and life, and the continuing work of grace as a person responds to Christ. At the heart of John Wesley's preaching and teaching: "For by grace you have been saved through faith, and this is not your own doing; it is the gift of God" (Eph 2:8). The phrase "making disciples of Jesus Christ" becomes a kind of summary statement of a much broader relationship that involves God in Christ, the Spirit of God, the testimony of a follower, and a receptive and responsive heart of another. It is all about the interaction and intersection of several participants under the power of divine, amazing grace and love. For our part, we are called to invite others into a redeeming and reforming relationship with Jesus, Lord and Savior, Son of God, Messiah. We invite, we encourage, we inspire, we share, and we summon people to follow Jesus. We proclaim in both word and deed the good news of God's love made visible in Jesus.

In recent years, the Council of Bishops has added a qualifying phrase "for the transformation of the world." The task of making, becoming, and living as disciples of Jesus is not about personal rewards, not about "me" and "mine" but more about (again) "your kingdom come . . . on earth" (Matt 6:2). It could be said that a disciple has not yet been *made* until that new disciple is engaged in the process of making another disciple, and serving together, along with the whole Body, for the transformation of the world in the image of Jesus. What is envisioned in this extension of the mission of the church is Wesleyan, and it is part of our faithful response to the call of God. It echoes these observations from George Hunter:

> I propose that we are called in our apostolic mission to love, serve, witness, and make disciples in every population sector . . . and to join in any and all common causes that help move society, or the world, more toward God's revealed purposes. . . . The integrity of organizations, institutions, and societies requires . . . that they remember their identity, their main business, their driving values, and their foundational ideas.[13]

This moment in time demands that we United Methodists recover and reclaim our evangelical heritage with a passion. Such a recovery is not about adding new members to the church rolls, although that will be an important and significant (and much needed) by-product. Such a reclaiming is not about losing any of the gains and progress that has been made in and for justice issues in the world. It is about remembering who we are and what we have been called to be and to do as baptized believers and followers of Jesus. It is about retrieving our Wesleyan roots and a passion for souls. In his 1756 "Address to Clergy," John Wesley spoke to those clergy who were concerned about higher salaries and better places to serve, to the neglect of the main purpose.

> [A] larger income does not necessarily imply a capacity of doing more spiritual good. And this is the highest kind of good. It is good to feed the hungry, to clothe the naked: but it is a far nobler good to "save souls from death," to "pluck" poor "brands out of the burning." And it is that to which you are peculiarly called, and to which you have solemnly promised to "bend all your studies and endeavors."[14]

We must become passionately and intensely committed to the task of making disciples—not for the sake of the institution but for the glory of God in Christ Jesus. If we are to move down the path from good to great, from dying to growing, then we must pay attention to the mandates of the Scripture from which we draw our inspiration and by which we shape our lives together. Three "great" passages recorded in the Gospel of Matthew shape our response and the direction for our disciple-making ministry.

THE GREAT INVITATION

The Great Invitation appears in numerous passages in the pages of Matthew, starting in chapter 4 as Jesus invites Peter and Andrew to come along: "Follow me" (v. 19). In chapter 9, Jesus invites Matthew to leave his old job: "Follow me" (v. 9). Again in chapters 16 and 20, others are invited to follow Jesus on a different road. Every time the invitation is extended, people are challenged to change their allegiance, their loyalty, their primary purposes, and follow Jesus: to Jerusalem, to the cross, and to life. This is the beginning of the movement, and is the foundation of a renewed Church for the twenty-first century. If we are not following Jesus, whom then are we following? If we are not taking our directions by traveling with Jesus on the road, whom, then, are we listening to? If we are not boldly and radically imitating Jesus in the way we live and make our decisions, then the gospel story is reduced to a cute little fairy tale with a happy ending—it makes a person feel good but has no power. The beginning of a passion for the souls of others begins in our own hearts. Then, as we are incorporated into the Body of Christ, other

> One of the factors contributing to the growth of our conference has been "the willingness of bishops and conference leadership to celebrate, embrace, and encourage the development of the 'large membership church!' There is, within our denominational system and within our culture, a negative bias toward growth, success, and largeness."
> (Jeff Spiller, Christ United Methodist Church, Mobile, Alabama)

travelers join us to support, encourage, and make the way bearable. However, our movement from good to great is only beginning.

THE GREAT COMMANDMENT

When we sign on to follow Jesus, when we are dripping with the waters of baptism, marking us as distinct, peculiar people, we embark on a journey of discovery. Perhaps the single greatest discovery we make is that found in Matthew 22: "You shall love the Lord your God with all your heart, and with all your soul, and with all your mind . . .You shall love your neighbor as yourself" (vv. 37-39). The person who posed the question that led to this response was, from all indications, a very religious person. Like us, the person probably struggled more with the meaning and application of this Great Commandment than with the memory work required to quote it and cite it. This Great Commandment captures the heart of Wesley's doctrine of perfection. In treatises, addresses, and sermons, Wesley constantly referred to love of God and neighbor as the mark of a Methodist, and the essence of perfection. Kenneth Collins writes about this perfect love in a commentary on Wesley's "Plain Account of Christian Perfection."

> Growing in grace on the way to perfect love is a *process* that Wesley explores in his writings in both a positive and a negative fashion. Positively speaking, the Holy Spirit becomes increasingly resident in the human heart such that the holy tempers of love are inculcated in a real and enduring way. . . . Negatively speaking, growth in holiness entails not simply the inculcation of holy love, but also the displacement of unholy tempers and affections, a radical, "cutting" work that results in nothing less than the death of the carnal nature.[15]

THE GREAT COMMISSION

The ordering and sequencing here is important. For us, beginning the journey with a commitment to follow Jesus is followed by learning to live and practice the love of God and neighbor in our actions. It is then, and only then, that we can hear and apply Matthew 28:19-20: "Go therefore and make disciples of all nations, baptizing . . . and teaching them to obey." If our distinctive Wesleyan emphasis on evangelism is to be reclaimed, we must hear and tell the whole story. No "great" passage can be isolated nor stand on its own, for each one informs and shapes the other. We must be deliberate and intentional about reaching out to all people, offering them Christ, inviting them into a personal relationship with Christ, incorporating them into the Body of Christ, and providing the opportunities for growth in the faith and ministry in the world. We must be clear that it is the gracious, merciful action of God that convicts and converts a heart, and that we are but the vehicles through which the experience of God's grace is offered. Again, it is John Wesley who helps us keep our thinking, our theology, and our actions straight. In a revealing passage in his fourth "discourse" on the Sermon on the Mount, Wesley writes (again, acknowledging the masculine language that was Wesley's time): "Though it is God only changes hearts, yet he generally doeth it by man. It is our part to do all that in us lies, as diligently as if we could change them ourselves and then to leave the event to [God]."[16]

In a distant past, in a very different context for this country, both camp meetings and revivals were effective means of reaching the people with the gospel of Jesus, of inviting people to follow, and of expressing love of God. Methodists led the way in pioneering these new events that transformed a continent. We are charged, now, with the responsibilities of discovering innovative ways of doing the same for this and future generations. Fresh perspectives and understandings of evangelism, seen and practiced from a holistic approach, are required. But we can no longer avoid or hide or neglect the ministry of evangelism. Listen to three voices setting out to define evangelism for the twenty-first century. Bishop Scott Jones writes that evangelism is "that set of loving, intentional activities governed by the goal of initiating persons into Christian discipleship in response to the reign of God."[17] Brad Kallenberg has written about the ministry of evangelism in a postmodern time: "[E]vangelism must be a corporate

> "One of the best ways a bishop or conference can begin to reverse the decline among churches is to promote the importance of the Great Commission. This can be taught, proclaimed, celebrated in local churches, modeled and even emphasized in training events." (Cory Smith, Woodland United Methodist Church, Montgomery, Alabama)

practice, executed by the community that is the source of the believer's new identity . . . must seek to assist [the paradigm] shift by being dialogical in style and by, wherever possible, enlisting potential converts in telling the story."[18] Laceye Warner suggests that evangelism refers to "those ministry activities that facilitate an individual's introduction to the gospel of Jesus Christ and initiation into the kingdom of God."[19]

With those voices as background, we must recognize that what is desperately needed today is a healthy, holistic understanding and practice of evangelism. The secular media has defined evangelism in a very narrow way, a kind of triumphalist, exclusive approach that caters to a segment of consumers looking for easy answers. On the other hand, far too many Methodists and other similar mainline Protestants have so diluted (or simply thrown out) the concept that it is relegated, if at all, to a small committee within the organization. What is required for this present age is nothing short of a recovery of the Wesleyan evangelical spirit and discipline that offers those outside the church an unapologetic claim about Jesus that affects both individual lives and the social structures of this world. As Jones, Kallenberg, Warner, and others urge: this is a *kairos* moment when we in the church, and in particular the Methodist movement, have an unprecedented opportunity to reach populations and generations that are estranged from the institutional church, yet intensely curious about all matters spiritual. Their voices sound consistent themes: intentional activities, carried out in the context of the Body, and grounded in the Reign or Kingdom.

We must recover the importance of being witnesses for Jesus Christ, building our witness around our friendship networks and personal relationships. We will have to find our voice and a vocabulary. The mantle of personal witness and testimony has been gathering dust in the back of the church attic for decades. This is not a task to be delegated only to the clergy or so-called professional evangelists. Rather, every baptized believer must reclaim the Acts 2 model of hitting the streets, telling the story out of one's own experience of following Jesus, and loving God and neighbor in concrete, caring ways. "I cannot judge or confess that a story that involves me is true unless the story shapes my life. To call a story true is to trust it to be a reliable guide for interpreting my past and navigating my future."[20] Thus, our witness must be done in authentic ways, growing out of our own personal experiences. Philippians 1:27 is a guiding word: "live your life in a manner worthy of the gospel of Christ." A major part of our personal witness is to allow people to see Jesus in our actions as well as in our words. And, to hear us point to Jesus as the source of our life, hope, and joy, with an invitation to join us on the journey. "Human beings are privileged to participate in God's saving acts. We do so as the church of Jesus Christ, and as individuals exercising our gifts to build up the church and participate in its mission."[21] We bear witness to the gracious action of God in Jesus to reconcile the world, to make new, and to restore life in all its fullness, in all its abundance. Several activities that can assist in such intentional evangelism and personal witness in this time include at least the following practices.

SMALL GROUPS

Small groups provide a place where people can be introduced to the demands of discipleship, the disciplines of faith, and the implications of following Jesus. These small groups can take place in a variety of settings, with a variety of covenants, but with a common goal of nurturing and developing a deeper, closer relationship with one another and with Christ. Such groups were a key component of the early Methodist movement and were part of the genius of John Wesley that clearly distinguished him from other renewal movements of his time.

PERCEPTIVE AWARENESS

Before we can be effective at introducing people to the saving, transforming grace of God in Jesus, we will have to know who they are, where they live, and how they currently think. Evangelism must start in the immediate neighborhood where a church building stands—be a witness for Jesus where you live, where you are located, even if the demographics have changed the population—*especially* if the demographics have changed the population makeup. Spend time and invest energy in knowing the neighbors, in loving the neighbors, and then in inviting them to experience life in and through Jesus.

EFFECTIVE COMMUNICATION

We have to learn to speak the language of the gospel in the context of the culture in which we find ourselves. We must connect with people where they live and learn twenty-first-century communication skills to reach this and future generations. This does not mean changing the message, watering it down, hiding the details of the cross, or pretending that the gospel is really pretty easy. It does mean telling the story, living the story, embodying the story, and inviting others to take their place in the story.

MEETING NEEDS

Effective evangelism is not just about speaking or preaching or telling the gospel story. The most effective evangelism for the twenty-first century will be found in meeting the needs, addressing the hurts, and healing the pain of individuals caught up in the tangle and confusion of this world that seems bent on destroying itself. As we get to know the neighbors, we also sense the pain, the need, and the concerns that dominate their lives. Modeling the Great Commandment may be one of the most effective ways of fulfilling the Great Commission. This is in our DNA as the latest generation of the Wesleyan movement. Again, Heitzenrater connects the dots for us and for our Wesleyan evangelical heritage:

> The Oxford Methodists in the early 1730's . . . spent a good deal of their time, money, and energy in a ministry of mercy to the poor—educating the children in the workhouses, taking food to the needy, providing wool and other materials from which people could make clothes and other durable goods to wear or sell. This particular emphasis on "love of neighbor" and following Christ's example ("who went about doing good," Acts 10:38) continued to characterize Methodism as it entered the revival.[22]

Will it continue to characterize us? Will we engage in the vital—though long neglected—ministry of evangelism, with a passion for the souls of people? Will we practice our evangelism, not with tract distribution or revivalistic scare tactics, but with genuine, authentic acts of love for neighbor? Will we go about doing good as we learn from Jesus, or will we keep it all to ourselves? Will we be unafraid to name the name of Jesus as the reason for the hope that is within us, and for our actions of meeting the needs of people, and working for justice issues in a world of injustice, violence, hatred, prejudice, and poverty? Will we follow, love, and go in the name of Jesus? Will we make disciples of Jesus for the transformation of the world—or be content to simply be good and quietly fade into the sunset?

BUT IT'S THE SOUTH AND THE BIBLE BELT

Serving God during these first years of the twenty-first century in the Alabama–West Florida Conference carries some stigmas and stereotypes. From other parts of the country, it is often said that this area is the beneficiary of the many people who are moving into this region from cold, northern areas and thus our growth comes at the expense of our neighbors. I also hear rather frequently that since we are in the South and that since the Bible Belt is still alive and well, that such talk of evangelism is a regional concern and culturally acceptable. If the Bible-Belt South is the label applied and the reason given for growth (thus to be dismissed by other parts of this country), then why is it that the Alabama–West Florida Conference has grown over the last thirty-five years and adjacent areas have not? Would it not stand to reason that if we are growing everyone else must be since we are all in a unique Southern culture? The reality is that except for the explosive population growth of large metropolitan areas in some of the surrounding states, United Methodists in the South do not fare any better than other regions of the country. There must be something else. It has also been suggested that because we are growing, we must somehow not be Wesleyan in our theology or methodology. I would counter that unless all of us are intentional in authentic, holistic evangelism, we are not Wesleyan. We absolutely must move beyond easy labels because to resort to such portrayal only weakens our complete witness for Jesus. I am convinced that what is called for today is nothing less than recovering Wesley's emphasis on perfect love, his investment of time and energy on behalf of the poor and the neglected, and his passionate focus on winning souls incorporate the best of who we can be as United Methodists.

Across the Alabama–West Florida Conference, we intentionally lift up, highlight, celebrate, encourage, or provoke churches to take seriously what we know as professions of faith—the new believers in our Acts 2 model. We are clear that this is one of the major factors in determining appointments of pastors, and in asking congregations to thrive by fulfilling the purpose for which they were called into existence in the first place. We have taught and modeled the importance of meeting human needs as a major factor in the ministry of evangelism. Whether those needs are about hunger and poverty, or relational challenges, or addictive behaviors, pastors and churches are engaged in providing places of hope and healing in the name of Jesus. And the name is named! George Hunter puts it this way: "I submit that evangelical Christianity is an apostolic movement entrusted both with the Lord's mandate to be 'fishers' of men and women and to make disciples among all peoples *and* the imperative to work for a just world for people . . . to live in."[23] If we are going to see a reversal of the downward spiral of membership, participation, and loyalty within The United Methodist Church—and other mainline denominations—we must reclaim our passion for the souls of people and boldly proclaim Jesus as Savior, *and* we must renew our compassion for the hurts of people and boldly offer hope, healing, and hospitality to all God's children. We must boldly invite people to once again experience God's grace and then stay with them as they—and we—deepen our commitment to discipline and service.

> **"I believe that a return to the Wesleyan tenet that the first and most important task is to bring people to know the Lord Jesus Christ and then to nurture them in that relationship. It is out of that relationship that any significant social and missional enterprises emerge, and without that relationship missional endeavors cannot be long sustained."**
> **(Joe Bullington, Fairhope United Methodist Church, Fairhope, Alabama)**

I am a regular subscriber and reader of the monthly magazine *Fast Company* and have been almost since it was launched in 1996. I collect them the way another generation accumulated *National Geographic*. The April 2003 issue of *Fast Company* had a feature article on Google, the Internet search engine, and those who founded it, run it, and keep it on the edge and growing.[24] Some of phrases used to describe the company and those who work there provide insights about the future of The United Methodist Church. For instance, working as an engineer for the company, the article says, requires "being both insanely passionate about delivering the best search results and obsessive about how you do that." Imagine what could happen within the church if clergy and lay became insanely passionate, even obsessive, about the gospel, God's reconciling love in Christ Jesus, for the world. That Google article went on to note that the engineers were also "frighteningly single-minded" and on a "quest for impossible perfection." Does that sound like a John Wesley of the twenty-first century? Finally, Peter Norvig, an engineering director is quoted in the article, "These are people who think they are creating something that's the best in the world. And that product is changing people's lives." Wow!

I happen to believe that the gospel of Jesus Christ is the greatest news to be offered to the world, and that it profoundly changes lives and has the power to transform the world. This gospel is good news of great joy for a confused, frightened world not because *we* dreamed it up, but because God's redeeming, transforming grace is the foundation and theme of the message. As Charles Wesley wrote in 1747: "Breathe, O breathe thy loving Spirit into every troubled breast."[25] Not only do we need to sing that and believe it, but we also need to act and serve as if this news really is the best for all people, in all parts of the world. Unfortunately, much of what happens in the life of some churches is geared toward status quo, maintaining what we have where we are, biding our time, and settling for mediocrity. Being passionate about the gospel, being single-minded in our devotion to God, and being on a quest for perfection are all at the heart of our Wesleyan heritage. At this point in time, we can no longer afford to be boring or indifferent about this gospel. We must reclaim that heritage of passion for souls and fervor for holistic evangelism. As we do, we will be on our way, having turned the corner from good and dying to great and growing.

CHAPTER SEVEN

INNOVATION, FLEXIBILITY, AND THE CONNECTION

How do we turn the corner? Can we actually reverse the downward spiral of Methodism? We know that the status quo is unacceptable. We know that if we simply keep going on the road we are now traveling, we will continue to lose members, influence, and opportunities to significantly affect the world with the Jesus Way of grace and love. We know that we cannot continue to prop up a dying institution. We must free ourselves and our resources for ministry with the Kingdom vision of Jesus. But in order to do that, in order for a new church, a new world to be born, the old way must be relinquished. Can we find the will to make a different church and change our focus before we try to make a different world?

The denomination-institution as a whole has opted to keep doing what it has always done, making a few minor adjustments (primarily for financial reasons), shuffling a few programs in the name of cooperation, and continuing to try harder. Pronouncements, plans and projections, pastoral letters, and resolutions offered by the Council of Bishops are met with intense scrutiny, attempting to decipher which side won the argument and carried the day. General agencies have been relegated to a period of downsizing and positioning themselves for survival when the budget numbers are crunched and the apportionment dollars shrink. The General Conference passes numerous resolutions,

> "People come to worship, not to be impressed, but to be fed on the Bread of Life and not the preacher. Congregations gather not to see the preacher's light, but the light of Christ. They gather, not to see how much we have been inspired, but to be inspired. Churches in the Alabama–West Florida Conference are growing and the conference as a whole is growing because the gospel is being made personal, practical, understandable, and applicable. It is not a truncated gospel that makes you feel good, but the whole truth that confronts, challenges, encourages, convicts, informs, and enlightens." (Art Luckie, First United Methodist Church, Demopolis, Alabama)

many without serious conversation, but almost all with an eye toward various social issues. Of the 368 resolutions found in the 954 pages of the 2004 *Book of Resolutions* only one page even addresses the issue of evangelism, and none addresses the fact that the denomination is, if not dying, at least on life-support.[1] Instead of listening to the voices of those local churches that have grown in membership and participation *and* offered significant outreach ministry touching the lives of thousands of people with hope, we have created more bureaucracy and erected more ministry silos. We have rearranged the furniture, but it is still the same furniture. We rename pieces of the structure, but end up staying in our comfortable ruts and prolonging (sometimes accelerating) the downward spiral. It is difficult to change and radically remake an institution when that institution is built on taking sides and living with labels; when it is satisfied with status quo and with mediocrity; when we protect turf and hold on to privileges and rights at the expense of the gospel. Yet I am absolutely convinced that all is not lost, that there is hope, and that the future can be radically different from the last fifty years. It is out of that conviction, out of my own personal experience of grace, mercy, and forgiveness, and out of the signs of hope that I see in many corners of the Church that I propose a direction forward for the denomination, whose Wesleyan theology I just happen to believe is what this twenty-first century world needs.

The previous chapters have sketched an outline of some crucial steps to be taken if any transformation is to occur, and if a radical revolution will once again send the people of the Methodist movement into the world to spread scriptural holiness, to make disciples, and to offer hope and healing in this fractured world. (1) Redefining and holding clergy accountable for effective, fruit-bearing ministry, (2) challenging local churches to grow, thrive, and become dynamic centers of mission and ministry, and (3) reclaiming our Wesleyan evangelical roots, without sacrificing the call to address justice issues in society are key elements in reforming, reshaping, and renewing the denomination. None of them directly address the ingrained bureaucracy and institutionalism that is The United Methodist Church today. To reverse the decline of this denomination, we must begin where it matters: with an intentional focus on the local church where all three of these elements of deep change can, will, and must affect the congregation. Strong, growing, local churches, connected in mission, make up a strong, growing annual conference; and strong, growing annual conferences reverse the downward spiral of the denomination.

I believe it can happen if we are willing to invest time, energy, resources, and excellent leadership into cultivating healthy, thriving congregations. That is our future. That is where our focus must be. As many have suggested, we cannot predict the future, but we can certainly reshape and create that future. For those of us in the church—whatever the denomination—that future is God's future. Are we willing to risk entering a revolution shaped by God's Spirit, knowing that God's future is the preferred alternative rather than the current declining mess? Lifting up God's preferred future, organizing ourselves to live into and out of that future, and altering our current trajectory are the challenges for the church and its leaders today. How do we get there? How do we get out of this slippery downward spiral?

INNOVATION AND CREATIVITY

If we are going to make such a significant course correction, one of the critical options that is before us is whether we will be creative and imaginative or maintain the same-old-same-old focus. We cannot continue to expect different results from doing the same thing. It is not only insanity; it is fatal. At the same time, the innovation required does not abandon nor neglect our roots. Even as the Scriptures remind us that God is in the business of doing new things, that newness is always anchored in God's own identity of love, mercy, and grace that empowers and that leads to new life, a new creation. The images of the psalm writers are vivid when referring to God as a rock, a shelter, and a fortress. At the same time, God is a wind, a breath, and a Spirit that moves to create new life out of death, to bring forth light out of darkness, and to be a way when there seems to be no way.

> "All growth is change, but not all change is growth. Where growth is happening, change is happening too. Being creative and loving are vital seed if an environment is to be formed that allows change to be planted and fruit to grow." (Ron Ball, Woodlawn United Methodist Church, Panama City, Florida, currently the Montgomery–Opelika District Superintendent)

Like other bishops of the church, I am invited to preach, teach, dedicate and celebrate in many places, traveling from one church to another on any given Sunday. I never quite know what to expect when I arrive. Will I be surprised by exciting, empowering worship? Or will I have to endure boring, uninspiring worship? Will I encounter people who get it, who have caught a vision of the Jesus way of life? Or will I meet those who are hanging on and hoping against hope that the bishop has not come to finally close their church building? With my first steps inside a church facility, I sense immediately if this is a church that is creative, flexible, and open to new movements of God's Spirit, or if it is a church that is satisfied with where it is, that is resting on its past glories, and that is closed to any possibility of God showing up among them. At one extreme, I often find an order of worship that is tired, routine, and lifeless, and copied on bulletin covers right out of the 1960s. The music, played on an out-of-tune piano, is offered with the enthusiasm of a funeral dirge. The congregation knows precisely when to stand or sit, mouths words of prayers or hymns or creeds with no enthusiasm for the bold, powerful message they dare record. Feeble efforts at so-called contemporary worship are not always an improvement, with poor musicians, songs that the leaders enjoy but no one else sings and routines that are known to the insiders but not necessarily to the visitors. A lazy duplication of some canned program or sermon series that was purchased over the Internet because it worked in some megachurch somewhere (forget theology) does not infuse life or light to anyone. At another level, I often find an average, perhaps even above-average church and pastor. For a variety of reasons, however, they have chosen to settle for mediocrity and status quo, when the potential for worship services and ministry options to soar are apparent. Going along with the flow seems a much more comfortable option than a bold step into the future, even if such a decision opts for following Jesus as opposed to maintaining an institution.

That we live in a very different world and that Christendom as an organizing principle is dead are not reasons to dissect what went wrong or to point fingers at easy targets to blame for our decline. The gospel has not changed! The character of God and the call of Jesus remain the same! The urgency of the moment demands that we find creative ways to embody our faith tradition in ways that communicate and connect with people who live in the twenty-first century. To be creative in this kind of world demands that our churches and our laypeople and clergy leaders decide that what matters most is people—the very ones loved by God and for whom Jesus gave himself. Churches must find ways to organize and structure the life of the church so that the institution is stable but is not the main or only thing that occupies time and energy. We should give permission to our churches to put together a plan that works for them, provided it is anchored in the love of God and does not violate the covenant of who we are as Wesleyans. Getting the word out, meeting needs, and embodying the gospel take precedence over getting the structure right and aligned with the bureaucracy. We must constantly push forward to discover the best and to embrace the new thing God is doing, and to which God is calling us. Even as we push forward in an environment of relentless change, there are some basic affirmations we must claim.

First, there are some pieces of our tradition we dare not let go of or change. As baptized believers and Jesus-followers, we must reaffirm the core of our faith. The Incarnation, Crucifixion, and Resurrection are essentials to our identity, our mission, and our purpose as individuals and as a church. These core beliefs form the foundation upon which we build now and into the future. That "in Christ God was reconciling the world" (2 Cor 5:19) is an affirmation of who God is and what God does in us and for us, as well as an invitation to a new life and a new way of being in the world. That Jesus Christ is Savior, Lord, and Redeemer is the unique, wonderful good news that fundamentally changes life, transforms communities, and creates hope and healing for hurting people in a troubled world.

Second, we can celebrate the past while focusing on the future. The heritage that is ours from John Wesley shapes how we understand and proclaim the good news (there is a reason we are not Calvinists!) and guides how we organize ourselves as a church (there is a reason we are connected!). But that heritage does not need to tie our hands or our imaginations for the future. Reinterpreting, reapplying, and renewing those connections open the door for exciting engagement with the twenty-first-century world. The twenty-first-century *connection* is much more about theology and mission than replicated organizational patterns that sap energy and misplace resources. The twenty-first-century *connection* is much more church-to-church networking for learning and encouragement than top-down bureaucratic programs that do little more than generate resentment and foster mistrust.

Third, being grounded in the strong traditions and heritage of our faith, and altering or amending the practices that have outlived their effectiveness, we are called into God's future. We believe that God has brought us thus far, and we are confident that God will take us into the future with hope. The message and core of the faith must not be compromised, but the way we share that message and the way we organize for effective ministry in a changed world requires bold new steps forward. Leaders must welcome change as a sign of God's new movement in the world and must invite the church to move into that future, which will require radically different ways of living and having our being. Andrew Cosslett, CEO of InterContinental Hotels, suggests that "people need to know why we are here and how we are going to win. Asking them to be motivated by financial goals just doesn't cut it. They need a higher-order quest. Without a compelling story, leadership becomes exhortation."[2] That quest, that compelling story, *is* the gospel. What are the steps required of a church and its leadership to move into the future with innovation and creativity?

CATERING TO THE MASSES

When the May 2006 issue of *Fast Company* arrived on my desk, my initial thought was to dismiss this particular issue. The cover featured a chef, and the lead articles appeared to be about cooking, restaurants, and other such items. I remember thinking there would be nothing of particular interest for me in this issue. As I quickly scanned the pages, I discovered an intriguing article entitled "Catering to the Masses" and, much to my surprise, found myself caught up in a story that not only bears telling but also carries important lessons for leadership, for the denomination, and for the future of our work and ministry.

Levy Restaurants provides the food concessions for some of the largest sporting events in the United States. Some of their clients include the Super Bowl, the National Basketball Association's All-Star Game, the World Series, NASCAR races, and, for the last few years, the Kentucky Derby. With attendance at some of those events surpassing the hundreds of thousands, I became keenly interested in how an organization could literally feed and care for that many people, in a short period of time, and in a confined area. The chef featured in the article was John Nicely, executive chef at the American Airlines Arena in Miami, Florida. It is in that arena that the Miami Heat professional basketball team plays home games, and recently play-off games, and the 2006 league championship. Every home game is a sellout with crowds of over nineteen thousand people. Nicely and his staff are responsible for providing "restaurant-quality meals and top-grade fast food to a sold-out stadium crowd—and to do it in the span of a couple of hours."[3] How does one deliver quality meals and service, on time, and with excellence? John Nicely suggests that it takes three things: outrageous preparation, relentless pursuit of creativity, and a knack for improvisation. It is that kind of excellence that is expected of him as a chef in the Levy Restaurant system that brings "fanatical attention to detail" and has its chefs "drilled not just in food prep but in the high art of resilience."[4] Those three qualities could become the hallmarks of the efforts and energy of the lay and clergy leadership of The United Methodist Church in the twenty-first century.

OUTRAGEOUS PREPARATION

Even if the menu does not change that much from game to game at the arena (hamburgers, hot dogs, shrimp), there is still an extensive amount of preparation that Nicely and his team must go through in order to have everything in its proper place and ready for the people who will attend the games and events. Such preparation includes knowing your customer, knowing what is consumed and what is left over, and knowing where all the team members and their expertise need to be in order to achieve success. In addition, the team members have to be sure that all the ingredients are on hand and ready for use, which means extensive inventory, counting, and planning ahead. The attention to detail may almost seem obsessive, but pulling off a major feat like serving that many people requires it.

For those who are called upon to serve God and lead the church, can we expect to do anything less than the same kind of *outrageous preparation?* This means we have to be intentionally prayerful and disciplined regarding who is on team. Jim Collins challenges every organization that would seek to move from good to great: "You start by focusing on the First Who principle—do whatever you can to get the right people on the bus, the wrong people off the bus, and the right people into the right seats."[5] No amount of preparation, however obsessive or outrageous, will be of much benefit if the wrong people are assigned to carry out the work. Our United Methodist system of guaranteed appointments perpetuates nice and good. However, if we can elevate the effectiveness of clergy leadership (chapters 3 and 4), if we can expect excellence from all leaders, and if we take seriously guaranteed accountability, we will have taken important first steps toward getting the right people in the right places to transform the denomination. Tending one's spiritual foundation and roots, immersing oneself in Scripture, constantly learning and growing in skills and abilities are basic components of *outrageous preparation* for clergy leaders.

Likewise, congregations must constantly be engaged in *outrageous preparation* to effectively serve, witness, and be in ministry in this present age. The Acts 2 church, according to Luke, "*devoted* themselves to the apostles' teaching" (Acts 2:42, emphasis mine), which is certainly more than an occasional appearance at a brief Sunday school class or sporadic attendance at weekly Bible study. Preparing to serve and cater to the masses requires in-depth study, a strong prayer life, intentional leadership training, and empowering encounters with God through worship. When churches have immersed themselves in the community, when they have discovered the needs of the people within their parish boundaries, and when they have clearly heard the call of God to feed the hungry, visit the sick, or clothe the naked, they will have started on a process of outrageous preparation to become a dynamic, thriving place of ministry. This is not for the weakhearted or lazy-boned, but is an *outrageous preparation* of heart, soul, and mind.

RELENTLESS PURSUIT OF CREATIVITY

John Nicely and his team in Miami know that unless they find bold new ways of preparing and presenting the food, the public will grow restless and bored. The corporation understands that preparing routine meals in paper wrapping will not keep and maintain an admiring, appreciative public. "Levy encourages a hunger for new ideas. Once a year, it holds a culinary, beverage, and service Olympics to identify new ideas and best practices across facilities. . . . It runs an innovation kitchen in Chicago . . . [and] stresses quality and creativity."[6] The base meal may still be the same, but the creativity, the originality, the imagination, and the innovation will be experienced as exciting and enticing. This point was made even more visible to me recently when I watched a food delivery truck unloading inventory at a fast-food restaurant not necessarily known for creativity or taste. The truck then left that parking lot and pulled across the street to a significantly upscale restaurant, well-known for higher prices and quality food—same truck, many of the same ingredients, and yet different results when the food was placed in front of the customer.

For clergy leaders and for churches, the *relentless pursuit of creativity* should be standard operating procedure. This has everything to do with offering an exciting, empowering word of hope that touches the lives of people in the real world. What is sadly lacking in too many churches and among too many leaders is an incredible lack of innovation and imagination. We keep doing church (from the local level to the national level) the way we were taught. The very idea of being creative, of taking the message and allowing it to soar with different tones or melodies seems to have a whole host of naysayers. "The old time religion is good enough for me," some good church members announce as another church closes or more young families leave. Any change, any creative or innovative movement, creates discomfort and, thus, is too quickly dismissed. What if we held innovation seminars where best practices and creative ideas were shared, explored, and implemented? What if we were not so suspicious and critical of those whose creativity and innovation results in growing churches, expanding mission outreach, and a renewed and dynamic Wesleyan movement? What if we found ways to connect with each other in order to learn and support one another?

The church has been entrusted with the message of new life and new hope for individuals and for our world, a message that is revealed in Jesus but that is a consistent theme coursing its way through the Scriptures. The imagery of creativity and music is an underlying theme throughout *The Art of Possibility*, primarily because one of the authors, Benjamin Zander, is conductor of the Boston Philharmonic Orchestra. The Zanders write creatively about letting life soar, and for us in the church, sharing, telling, living, and embodying the message with a *relentless pursuit of creativity*.

> Life flows when we put our attention on the larger patterns of which we are a part, just as the music soars when a performer distinguishes the notes whose impulse carries the music's structure from those that are purely decorative. Life takes on shape and meaning when a person is able to transcend the barriers of personal survival and become a unique conduit for its vital energy. So too the long line of the music is revealed when the performer connects the structural notes for the ear, like a bird buoyed on an updraft.[7]

Imagine what might be if clergy and lay became unique, creative conduits for the vital energy of the gospel, witnesses buoyed by the updraft of the Spirit of God blowing in serendipitous ways.

KNACK FOR IMPROVISATION

"No matter how diligently Levy prepares, it can't control everything. . . . Without fail, there are surprises, and Levy's ability to improvise is critical."[8] John Nicely tells stories of always having to be ready for the unexpected: "a shortage of cashiers, a cash-register glitch . . . a run on roasted potatoes."[9] What do you do when one concession stand runs short of a certain item of food and another is overstocked? How do you make connections and improvise a solution? Although they may appear to be making it up as they go, there is order in the confusion, a foundation and a base from which the team does not vary. Their outrageous preparation and teamwork are what holds them together yet allows them flexibility and the ability to improvise immediately, responding to an urgent need or looming crisis.

If our denomination is to remake itself, revitalize its life, and reform its future, we will have to learn to practice the faith, but not enshrine it; we will have to learn to improvise along the way, but not deviate from the core; we will have to innovate and respond, but not ignore and forget. Certainly we will understand, appreciate, and affirm the habits that have been formed in us and for us in Scripture and Wesleyan tradition, but we will also understand, appreciate, and affirm the practices that may be called for, even improvised, in response to current reality or the experience of God's Spirit moving in us in this present age. To be flexible, innovative, and improvisational means that we understand the core business in which we are engaged, and that we live it out faithfully in a variety of contexts and settings.

INTO THE FUTURE

Stephen Covey suggests that for any organization to make a significant difference in the world there are three qualities that must be present: vision, discipline, and passion. These same three themes are consistently lifted up as critical by other writers, consultants, and coaches as organizations look to become great or excellent. These same three themes are the foundation from which Levy Restaurants and, in particular, John Nicely can cater to the masses with creativity, innovation, and quality. Covey may have best painted the picture of how these three are embodied in his observation about Nelson Mandela.

Nelson Mandela, former president of South Africa, spent almost twenty-seven years in prison for fighting against the apartheid regime. Mandela was impelled by his imagination rather than his memory. He could envision a world far beyond the confines of his experience and memory, which included imprisonment, injustice, tribal warfare and disunity. Deep within his soul resonated a belief in the worth of every South African citizen.[10]

What might yet happen in The United Methodist Church with such a compelling vision leading, motivating, and inspiring us to reverse our downward spiral and to boldly proclaim and live the message of hope in and through Jesus? What if we were, finally, impelled more by our imagination, innovation, and improvisation than we were by the traditionalisms that stifle us and prevent us from engaging the world and its people with the power of divine love, the healing balm of mercy and compassion, and the life-giving grace of God?

> **"I think there is just no substitute for passion. This spiritual quality is hard to measure empirically, but passion is obvious and contagious where it burns. Before anyone is sent out to start a new church, we should put them in a locked room and tell them a new church plant is on the other side of the wall. Only those who gnaw their way through should get to start a new church."** (Doug Pennington, Lynn Haven United Methodist Church, Lynn Haven, Florida)

We live with change on a daily basis, whether it is in the realm of technology and gadgets, the world of politics, or the business-industrial world. The opening decade of the twenty-first century has witnessed chaotic change, mushrooming in time and space, and demanding more adjustments and adaptations from humans than perhaps ever before in history. Meanwhile, the church slowly and grudgingly admits current reality but seems much more content with its status quo and mediocrity. For some local churches, for some clergy leaders, and for some members of the bureaucratic institution, the idea of changing much of anything is tantamount to heresy. However, if The United Methodist Church is going to be a viable movement in the future, if the church is going to be alive and vital beyond the midpoint of the twenty-first century, and if the church is going to intentionally make disciples who are actively working to make a different world, some things will have to change. Business as usual can no longer be an option. The declining and aging membership rolls, the shrinking percentage of financial resources given to keep the institution functioning, and the frustration with and mistrust of national or general bureaucratic agencies contribute to the urgency of this moment. However, this does not mean that those of us entrusted with the treasure at the beginning of this century can simply resign and watch the candlewick slowly go out. That does not mean that such an end is inevitable. I am absolutely convinced that there is hope, a transforming hope that will reinvigorate the Wesleyan movement in this country through The United Methodist Church. It is a hope that can stop the hemorrhaging and restore us to a vital, dynamic, and growing church driven by a vision of boldly proclaiming and embodying scriptural holiness with such excitement and urgency that others will be inspired to join us on the way to life, and that radically transforms this world.

CHAPTER EIGHT

KEEPING HOPE ALIVE

In one of his series of small books ("essentials" he calls them), Tom Peters distills the essence of some of his other writings. *Leadership* now occupies a reserved place on my desk for quick reference. Early on in this book Peters speaks of hope. "The experts say Roosevelt was not much of an economist. And that Churchill was a questionable talent as military strategist. Yet they kept hope alive. 'A leader,' Napoleon famously said, 'is a dealer in hope.'" Peters continues by affirming a statement from John Gardner, who "echoes that Napoleonic dictum: 'The first task of a leader is to keep hope alive.'"[1]

Within the world of United Methodism and other mainline Christian bodies today, the need to keep hope alive is an urgent one. Given the downward spiral of so many of these denominations, and given the general drift of culture away from institutional religion, the need to keep hope alive is critical. My intent in raising the issues and concerns discussed within these pages is to point toward a particular hope. Although there are many signs of the demise and dysfunction of the system that is called United Methodist, there is yet hope. Out of chaos emerges order. Out of the wilderness comes new life. Out of crisis is born opportunity. The ancient prophet Habakkuk sounds the note of hope with clarity:

Though the fig tree does not blossom,
  and no fruit is on the vines;
though the produce of the olive fails
  and the fields yield no food;
though the flock is cut off from the fold,
  and there is no herd in the stalls,
yet I will rejoice in the LORD;
  I will exult in the God of my salvation.
God, the Lord, is my strength;
  he makes my feet like the feet of a deer,
  and makes me tread upon the heights. (Hab 3:17-19)

That is how the book of the prophet Habakkuk ends. Even though everything is collapsing, even though everything relied upon for livelihood and income is failing, and even though there does not appear to be much hope on the horizon, hope is there. It is to be found with the God of salvation, the God of hope, the God of creation, the God of all. Those of us who live within the new covenant will boldly add that this is also the living God, who is revealed and made known to us in Jesus and who continues to empower the faithful ones in the Spirit.

In an article published in 2004 by *The Christian Century*, theologian Miroslav Volf reflected on the lasting impact of Jurgen Moltmann. Moltmann's mid-twentieth-century seminal work on a theology of hope shaped a generation of church leaders. Volf wrote that

> one of Moltmann's lasting contributions . . . was to insist that hope, unlike optimism, is independent of people's circumstances. Hope is not based on the possibilities of the situation and on correct extrapolation about the future. Hope is grounded in the faithfulness of God and therefore on the effectiveness of God's promise. . . . Optimism is based on the possibilities of things as they have come to be; hope is based on the possibilities of God irrespective of how things are. Hope can spring up even in the valley of the shadow of death.[2]

From the prophet Habakkuk, through the revelation of Jesus, forward to Napoleon and Gardner, to Moltmann and Volf, the message is the same. Even in the midst of uncertainty and turmoil, there is yet hope. The invitation in this book is to transform our understanding of hope and allow that hope to transform us from hand-wringing and finger-pointing to making strategic choices and intentional decisions about our future as a denomination, starting at the most basic level: the local church. The hope that springs up from the grace and love of God will yet transform our ways of *doing* church and *being* Christian. Transforming hope allows us the opportunity to recover our sense of being a movement, on a mission in the world, rather than an institutional bureaucracy trying to survive for a few more decades. The church, the Body of Christ, should know and practice this transforming hope, for we are people who have been called, shaped, and sent in the joy of the Resurrection.

The Resurrection bursts upon us as a message of hope and a promise of God's power overcoming the darkness and turning defeat into triumph. For Easter people, this is not relegated to a one-day-per-year holiday complete with sunrise services and brass horns. Resurrection is an experience that radically transforms our lives and renews our spirits. When it becomes more than a story or a lesson to be read and sung, the Resurrection shatters our routines, points us toward God's future, and beckons us to walk a new way, making our life-decisions in the light of that glorious event. The women who went to the tomb on

> **"Be positive to the point of fault. The challenge is providing a 'hopeful' vision each step of the way. This is not always easy but always essential. I have found the challenge to be hopeful even in the face of difficult circumstances is the number one requirement."** (Philip McVay, Cokesbury United Methodist Church, Pensacola, Florida)

that first day of the week were on a routine mission of tending to the dead, following the burial customs of their day. The rest of the believers were hiding in a room paralyzed with the fear that either they would be arrested, or that everything they had staked their lives on for the previous few months had been futile. There seemed to be no hope. The announcement and evidence of the Resurrection shook them all. It still does. And it must, if we are to do anything other than tend to death and if we are to overcome our paralysis of fear that keeps us locked into the way we have always done things.

The Resurrection upsets our efforts to control and manufacture church. Just when the authorities thought they were finished with Jesus, the power of God broke through in an astounding way. No matter how carefully we plan things, put things in place, organize, expand, and maintain the institution, or arrange our schedules, God is still breaking through with hope that transforms and challenges us to engage in out-of-the-tomb practices. The Resurrection serves as a powerful reminder that we are, none of us, in this faith movement for the salary or the glory or the prestige or the office or the size of the church. We are placed in this moment and in this life for the sake of the One who calls us, gifts us, and sends us into the world to proclaim good news. We are dealers in hope—hope that transforms lives, transforms creation, and may just transform the church in the twenty-first century.

A FRAMEWORK—AND A WAY FORWARD

"What framework will transform us? What can we invent that will take us from an entrenched posture of hostility to one of enthusiasm and deep regard?"[3] This is a leap of faith that we desperately need to make: from entrenched postures to enthusiasm, from institutional maintenance to inspired ministry, from us versus them to deep regard and common mission, from static organization to movement. The United Methodist Church started as a movement within the Church of England, spread across the

North American continent, became an influential denomination that scattered around the globe, but now (at least in the United States) is limping into the twenty-first century. However, since we are Easter people who boldly proclaim the joy of the Resurrection and the transforming hope in Jesus, we do not have to succumb to any self-fulfilling prophecy of doom, gloom, and demise. Granted, the dismal statistics and the lack of energy within the membership, and the inward-turning, turf-protecting, self-perpetuating bureaucracy do not offer much hope for the future. In the words and phrases of Patrick Lencioni, we must discover a way to "rebuild reputation . . . fix our relationships . . . rebuild morale."[4] Where is that path, and what must we do to walk it? How do we move from an entrenched "way it is" mentality to an empowered "way forward" spirit? What framework will fundamentally change the life and movement of Methodism?

Along our journey together in the previous chapters, we have explored three areas to "rebuild our credibility,"[5] and build a framework for the future that is based on a hope that transforms: congregations that are vital and dynamic; clergy who are Christ-centered, excellent, and effective leaders; and a holistic Wesleyan evangelical theology. Although recognizing and acknowledging the deep downward spiral of United Methodism, I am still hopeful that our future does not have to be like our past. Even in the midst of the darkness that has gripped and threatened the institutional survival of this portion of the Methodist family, there are glimmers of hope and rays of light.

The Alabama–West Florida Conference is one of those—and there are others. The fact that one area, one conference, can show a sustained net growth of members and mission outreach while the rest of the denomination is sinking is a point of light and hope. The people who make up the membership of the churches of this conference have provided me glimpses and experiences of the God who continues to do amazing things through the congregations, in the communities. While growing in membership, the conference has expanded its global outreach through creative, energetic, and generous partnerships with the people of Russia, Ecuador, and Cameroon. While gaining additional worship participants, the conference has prophetically addressed significant justice issues including racism and poverty. While being on the cutting edge of starting new churches, the conference has embraced a more diverse population and broken down walls that for too long divided and that marginalized or categorized others. We have started churches in growing, urban population areas, and in deserted, inner-city buildings, we have intentionally reached out to new immigrant populations, we have invested in college ministries and encouraged young persons to respond to a call from God for service and ministry, we have relocated and rebuilt and expanded existing churches, we have been on the front edge of the curve toward multisite congregations, and we have discovered incredibly gifted people to serve in a variety of settings—from beach ministry on Panama City Beach to rural ministry in some of the poorest counties of these two states and in the nation; from megachurches with more than two thousand in worship on Sundays to small membership churches networking together to provide creative cooperative ministries in sparsely populated areas, from hurricane-ravaged recovery and rebuilding ministry to providing food and shelter for displaced, homeless persons. The churches of this area demonstrate the balance that is wonderfully and uniquely held together in our Wesleyan tradition: works of piety and works of mercy, inward and outward fruit, personal and social holiness. It is in that convergence, and in recovering the spirit that created a movement, that we find a transforming hope for our denomination. It is only as that Wesleyan spirit becomes more than an affirmation we recite or a treatise analyzing Mr. Wesley that we will discover a new day of hope: not mere words on paper but actual practices and habits in the life of the real world.

In the midst of the turmoil and chaos that surrounds us, in a complex and turbulent world where people too quickly resort to violence and terror, and in the uncertainty of constant and continuous change, the church of Jesus must speak, model, and offer hope and healing. For The United Methodist Church, at this moment in time, given current reality, do we have the will to radically reshape and refocus this denomination around a transforming hope? Are we willing to engage in what Robert Quinn calls "deep change" in order to reverse the decline and restore credibility?

It is much easier to focus on solving today's problems than it is to mold the future. It is easier to be an operational analyzer and taskmaster than it is to be a developmental and visionary motivator. Yet transformational leaders can do both. They link the operational present with the developmental future.[6]

What might that developmental future look like for The United Methodist Church? How might the three areas already addressed (congregation, clergy, and Wesleyan theology) be integrated into a new system and new way of being church? What innovative bold steps must be taken to move us into God's preferred future? Can we merge creative twenty-first-century models of leadership and organizational strategy with first-century, Acts 2 models of church, alongside eighteenth-century Wesleyan theology?

"Our pastors for the most part have proclaimed the Wesleyan emphasis upon a personal relationship with the Lord Jesus Christ as the foundation for faith and ministry. In addition, they have challenged the people to become involved in meaningful ministries, and significant things have been accomplished in our communities." (Joe Bullington, Fairhope United Methodist Church, Fairhope, Alabama)

The answers will be found in bold initiatives that would fundamentally change the institution of The United Methodist Church. This book can only scratch the surface. It is an invitation to move us away from optimistic thinking that believes and tells itself that all is well, that we can keep doing the same things we have always done, and that it is permissible to be a

131

dysfunctional, dying church. It is an invitation to a conversation that is centered on the transforming hope of God's grace, mercy, love, and power to renew, reform, and revolutionize the church and the world. Time is of the essence. We cannot prolong the decisions while we study the life and energy out of them, analyzing every angle and nuance for the next eight to twelve years—we do not have that luxury. We cannot go about business, or church, as usual and expect different results. That insanity is what has brought us to this moment in the first decade of the twenty-first century. Again as Robert Quinn demonstrates so well, no deep change will occur within any organization until deep change occurs within the person, the leader, the membership.

Wherever the apostle Paul traveled, he either started a revival or a revolution, in many cases both. As The United Methodist Church journeys into the twenty-first century, a radical reorienting of the entire system (a revolution) and a reconnecting with our Wesleyan heritage (a revival) must be instigated. Some of the decisions will be conscious choices made by the leadership or by the denomination through action of the General Conference; all of the decisions must be inspired by, empowered by, and driven by the Spirit of God invading the hearts and souls of the lay and clergy leaders. Can we become the Body of Christ in creative and transformative ways in the world? Are we willing to make bold moves—not incremental adjustments that amount to the deck-chair shuffle, but transformational change that will radically alter who we are, what we do, and where we go? This book points toward a transforming hope by going deep into the soul and passion of clergy leaders, into the self-identity and purpose of the local church, and into our Wesleyan evangelical heritage. The discussion and choices placed before us must be part of a system-as-a-whole repositioning and reallocating of resources. To decide to do nothing and continue as we are is a formula for continued dysfunction and death. To delay the choices is to prolong the downward spiral and risk losing what is left of any viability.

DEALERS IN HOPE

To solidify any deep change in The United Methodist Church, a complete institutional makeover will be required, including the role and function of the general church (our national bureaucratic institution). Since we have not heeded such calls of the last two decades, it may already be too late. This is precisely why the focus of the changes advocated here has been on local churches, clergy leaders, and Wesleyan theology rather than addressing the system at a national level. We must first grow deep, and then branch out: *after* the root system has been restored and is bearing fruit, *after* the foundation is solid and firm, *after* the infrastructure is well in place. When we have undergone deep change in the lives of the leaders and our local churches, transformation will surface through the organization, from district, to annual conferences, to general agencies, and to bishops. This is precisely why the theme verse that appears at the beginning of this book, and again here reads: "The surviving remnant of the house of Judah shall again take root downward, and bear fruit upward" (2 Kgs 19:30). The surviving remnant of United Methodism must focus on its root system that will then bear fruit in the transformation of the denomination and of the world.

However, following the insights of Robert Quinn and his invitation to deep personal change, there is one level of general leadership that must step forward: the Council of Bishops. As a bishop, I know all too well that I cannot serve in this office as was done a quarter century ago. The world has changed, the current reality of the denomination has changed, so I must change, and the council as a body must change.[7] The Council of Bishops of The United Methodist Church finds itself in an interesting time: called upon to lead in a season when authentic leadership is resisted and prophetic voices are stifled and dismissed with suspicion. At every level of society, people "yearn for a leader who can align the internal and external realities and make the organization successful."[8] Within The United Methodist Church, leadership takes its most visible form in the office of the bishop, extended through superintendents, who are appointed by the bishop to smaller geographic regions known as districts. In a world that is increasingly flat and decentralized, what should the role of the bishop and that of the district superintendent look like going forward? Rather than engaging in a debate with or a response to the various discussions and study commissions around the office of the bishop, I pose a different question. Most of those conversations and studies seem to be driven more by money and geography than by mission and possible growth strategies. However, what can and should the clergy and congregational leaders expect from their bishop?

During its thirty-five-year trend of membership growth, the Alabama–West Florida Conference experienced two different models of residential episcopal leadership. The growth of the conference can be traced to the mid-1970s when the annual net increases of membership, worship attendance, and mission involvement began. Until 1988 the Alabama–West Florida Conference *shared* a bishop with the North Alabama Conference. Prior to 1988, the bishop lived in Birmingham (North Alabama Conference) and maintained a presence in the southern tier of the state and northwest Florida through frequent visits, the district offices, and the conference headquarters building. This type of absentee, or nonresident, episcopal leadership did not negatively affect the growth and ministry of the conference. It was, in fact, during this time, when the bishop lived outside the bounds of the conference that the steady growth trend began.

Then, in the fall of 1988, having grown to a membership sufficient to sustain an episcopal office on its own, the Alabama–West Florida Conference was assigned its first residential bishop and embarked on a journey of carving out new relationships and learning new models of leadership. The positive growth continued. This suggests that the questions and issues that are debated across the denomination regarding geography and a *resident* bishop are misplaced. Ultimately, it is not about where a bishop lives, or how much territory a bishop must cover. The denomination should expect of its bishops that the whole Council will be *dealers in hope*. It must always be about the mission and vision, about motivation and inspiration, about creating an environment and an expectation of growth and vitality in every church that finally makes a difference. The focus of the conversation should be on coaching and developing clergy leadership and encouraging healthy, thriving churches where baptized believers serve God in the name of Jesus. It must be more about casting a vision than maintaining institutional stability in the office of a bishop who *resides* in a certain place. Rather than clarify expectations and qualities of a leader for the church in this time, we enter into arguments and set our agendas based on how many bishops there should be or what the salary and expense caps should be. The church needs leaders, but the duties and responsibilities of a bishop as listed in paragraph 414 of *The Book of Discipline* (2004) are, for the most part, about management.

There are many lists and extensive commentaries on the qualities of leaders for the twenty-first century, whether inside the church or within society. Characteristics that are common across all sectors and all institutions, including the church, include at least the following items. These should be minimal expectations for those who are elected to lead the church.

- *Relational.* The bishop-leader who is an autocratic, dictatorial, or unilateral decision-maker is outdated. The age of the collaborator and team builder is upon us. Bishops must forge partnerships with lay and clergy across the conferences, and that means investing time and energy into those relationships. To build those relationships, a bishop must be visible and present throughout the area to which she or he is assigned.
- *Visionary.* The leader grasps, interprets, and articulates the big picture of where an area, through its churches, is going. Discerning where God's Word and Spirit are intersecting with current reality provides the clues to new direction for a conference and a denomination. This means that casting, clarifying, and modeling the vision becomes paramount in the work of the bishop.
- *Strategic.* The leader works tirelessly to ensure that the organization, in whatever design emerges, is a reflection of the how the vision gets lived out and then shapes the whole. The bishop

must be a designer and strategic thinker, and must motivate others to help shape the future.

- *Coaching.* The leader is always discovering new persons to be mentored and coached for future leadership. There may be no more important role for the bishop-leader than to coach and equip the next generation of believers and followers.
- *Spiritual.* The leader is grounded, self-differentiated, and centered in Christ. The spiritual leadership offered is not about the office or the privileges, but always about following Jesus. Out of that spiritual depth grows new life, honesty, and vulnerability, and the commitment to lead out of a deep center.
- *Prophetic.* The leader is a risk taker and is confident that at the end of the day the mission will be accomplished.

The church should expect the bishops to embody and practice qualities such as these in their leadership. Like all clergy leaders, bishops must be growing in each of these areas and becoming more and more the persons loved, called, equipped, and sent by God and by the church. To live into, and live up to, these expectations, the bishop-leader should be clear that we are not simply to maintain and prop up an outdated system, but to energize and mobilize the disciple-believers in every place to be witnesses for Jesus and to be in mission in the world. The last thing the church needs is to perpetuate an old-style managerial system that hinders the movement of God in and for the world ("it is okay as long as we can control it") and stifles the creative empowerment of the Spirit ("it is possible but only if it has already been done").

In order to rehearse these components of leadership, I have been learning an important lesson about building relationships and fostering partnerships with strong, vital, growing, healthy churches. Concepts such as *collegiality* and *partnership* and *collaboration* must be more than theoretical. We cannot say we will work together and create teams, and then act in arbitrary, autocratic ways when it comes to appointments and itinerancy. Thomas Friedman is right on target in suggesting that in the emerging flat world the old-model, chain-of-command, top-down style of organizational leadership is being replaced with connections, networks, and relationships as primary foci. "When the world starts to move from a primary vertical (command and control) value-creation model to an increasingly horizontal (connect and collaborate) creation model . . . it affects everything."[9] In my role as bishop, this new, connect-and-collaborate model is being lived out as coach and visionary and missionary and encourager. I am learning that this horizontal model means that I have to partner with and trust the insights and dreams of local church pastors who have demonstrated excellence in leadership and building up the Body. This collaborative, consultative style does nothing to undermine the authority of the office of bishop, and if anything enhances it and extends it in support of the mission of the church.

When Christ United Methodist Church in Mobile, Alabama, wanted to bring a staff person on board for the express purpose of serving for twelve to eighteen months and then launching a new congregation in the community, I was not only excited but also supportive. This would be an opportunity to forge a creative partnership between the conference and a local church to extend the mission of Jesus in that community. The Cabinet and I (mainly me) had picked two persons we believed would be the right person; I leaned toward one in particular. Jeff Spiller has been the pastor of Christ United Methodist Church since 1979; he is the founding pastor of this amazing church that now numbers over forty-five hundred members with twenty-two hundred in attendance. Jeff believed he had found the right person, who happened not to be the one the superintendents and I were leaning toward.

"Growth in commitment is more important than numbers of spectators (persons who are not involved beyond attending a worship service). The stewardship of persons who are with God and others in ministry is vital." (Al Harbour, First United Methodist Church, Eufaula, Alabama)

> **Bishops should "be a model of spirituality and commitment by living the call to the episcopacy; offer growth opportunities for pastors; challenge barren churches to effectiveness by supporting the declining and small membership churches with pastoral and laity training in outreach; offer enthusiasm, encouragement, and accountability."**
>
> **(Larry Bryars, Shalimar United Methodist Church, Shalimar, Florida)**

Now I have a choice: exercise my authority in the office of bishop or trust Jeff, who has built the church, who teaches in leadership schools across the connection, and who knows the area, the people, and the DNA of Christ United Methodist Church. Thankfully, I went with Jeff's vision. Christ United Methodist Church continues to grow and thrive; the new church is now approaching two hundred in worship in less than eighteen months under their pastor whom I appointed in partnership, collaboration, and consultation with Jeff. God is teaching me! I pray I am learning.

Bishops must be dealers in hope and transformational leaders who energize and equip the church in every place to serve God in the grand Wesleyan tradition of personal and social holiness and not get caught up in the authority of the office. As visionary servants of the risen Christ, bishops must *lead* the church in its mission of representing and imitating Jesus in order to ignite a movement for hope and healing in the world. Bishops must engage the church in creative and holistic ways of making and growing disciples who follow Jesus and practice the faith (Gal 5:6). We must create an atmosphere of and expectation for growth and extension of God's mission in the world. We must work diligently and urgently toward developing an atmosphere for growth and the extension of God's mission that effectively and energetically addresses the brokenness of this world. What should drive the conversation is the mission; what should keep the discussion in focus is the growth of the church, the movement of the Spirit, and the potential for new life. Deep spiritual renewal and transformation will occur only in collaborative partnerships around a common mission inspired and directed by God's Spirit: *spreading scriptural holiness—sharing God's love, making disciples of Jesus, and transforming the world.*

POWER IN THE CONNECTION

Albert C. Outler was one of the most insightful interpreters of John Wesley in the mid-twentieth century. His work shaped an entire generation of pastors and leaders in United Methodism. His vision of a church for the twenty-first century is captured in these words:

> Give us a church whose members believe and understand the Gospel of God's healing love of Christ to hurting men and women. Give us a church that speaks and acts in consonance with its faith—not only to reconcile the world but to turn it upside down! Give us a church of Spirit-filled people in whose fellowship life speaks to life, love to love, and faith and trust respond to God's grace. And we shall have a church whose witness in the world will not fail and whose service to the world will transform it.[10]

The United Methodist Church and other denominations are in serious trouble, having moved from mainline to sideline. For United Methodists, who we have become and how we are conducting ourselves does not yet reflect Outler's vision. We have not turned the world upside down but seem fully capable of tearing ourselves apart instead. Having been a district superintendent and now a bishop, I can testify that some of our churches have a spirit—but it is a spirit of contentiousness, envy, fear, and self-preservation, along with a resistance to change and a willingness to crucify anyone who suggests change. What I have witnessed in those places has not reflected God's Spirit of grace, mercy, and love.

Some of the strategies outlined in this book are designed to provoke systemic changes for the church in the twenty-first century. There is too much at stake to pass through a series of incremental changes, adjusting the size of boards or committees or promoting a new initiative. The critical question is whether or not The United Methodist Church can endure another round of institutional-structural changes if some of the deeper issues are not addressed. As Adam Hamilton, a United Methodist clergy-person serving in the Kansas City area has written:

> The deepest problems facing our society are at core spiritual problems . . . the real solution must address the condition of the human heart; it must break hearts of stone, transform hate into love, and offer healing and deliverance to those who are slaves to ideas or their upbringing or their addictions.[11]

Addressing those spiritual problems will not be met by tinkering with the structure, drafting a new statement on some pressing issue, or investing in small steps of incremental change. At the same time, the way we have been doing things for the last five decades has only led to the decline, the loss of influence, and a view from the spectator bleachers. Settling for mediocrity and maintaining the status quo only perpetuates and, in all likelihood, increases the speed of the downward spiral. Courageous choices must be made:

- A redefined role of the bishop as a transformational leader, not a manager of a dying institution; a dealer in hope, not a pre-server of the status quo
- A system of responsibility that challenges all clergy and lay leaders to bear fruit, especially for evangelism and mission outreach
- A foundational understanding of the local church as the place where disciple-making occurs, with benchmarks and clear expectations for each church
- A national commitment to the planting of new churches designed to reach new generations and new immigrant populations
- A reclaiming of the Wesleyan emphasis on holy living and holistic evangelism
- A passion and a compassion for offering hope and healing to all God's children

- A general-national church system to revolutionize the bureau-cracy and redirect the resources and energy of the whole denomination toward creating healthy, dynamic, vital congregations

Items such as these must be intentionally focused on people, not programs, and on relationships, not mere institutional survival. By engaging in these, by implementing them, and by focusing our prayers and practices on such habits, a new and renewed Methodist movement can be launched. It is happening in some places and among some areas of the denomination. It can happen for the whole church. We are called to practice and model love of God and love of neighbor, to make and become faithful disciples of Jesus; to grow in grace as fully formed and fully devoted followers of Jesus, to extend and accelerate the coming of God's kingdom on earth as in heaven, and to establish in every place new or renewed United Methodist Acts 2 churches—where new believers come to new life, where worship is inspiring and empowering, where mission outreach is a core practice of every member, and where signs and wonders are regularly celebrated.

When we have become absolutely clear about our common mission and vision, we will enlist millions of believers, empowered by the Spirit, to transform lives, whole communities, and, indeed, the entire globe. Such a transforming hope is challenging and energizing. Designing and aligning a new system to replace a tired one will require risk taking and courageous action on the part of the people called Methodist. "By achieving clarity about the number one priority in an organization, and by clearly identifying the defining and standard operating objectives that contribute to it, companies will give their employees far less reason to fear being pulled apart at the seams."[12] For The United Methodist Church, in reclaiming and living out of both personal and social holiness, in modeling and practicing both intentional evangelistic activities and prophetic social justice endeavors, we will find that our hope has been transformed and a transforming hope has grasped us in such a way that "at the name of Jesus every knee should bend . . . and every tongue should confess that Jesus Christ is Lord" (Phil 2:10-11).

NOTES

INTRODUCTION

1. More will be said about the Bible Belt region in chapter 6.

1. CURRENT REALITY: A CRISIS IN THE MAKING

1. Thomas L. Friedman, *The World Is Flat* (New York: Farrar, Straus, and Giroux, 2005), 282.

2. Daniel Wolpert, *Creating a Life with God: The Call of Ancient Prayer Practices* (Nashville: Upper Room Books, 2003), 161.

3. Jim Collins, *Good to Great* (New York: HarperCollins, 2001), 85.

4. Rosamund Stone Zander and Benjamin Zander, *The Art of Possibility* (New York: Penguin Books, 2000), 168.

2. CLICHÉS FOR MAINTAINING THE STATUS QUO

1. Patrick Lencioni, *Silos, Politics and Turf Wars* (San Francisco: Jossey-Bass, 2006), 176.

2. Ibid., 124.

3. Ibid., 142.

4. The Council of Bishops, "Our Shared Dream: The Beloved Community" (Nashville: The United Methodist Publishing House, 2003).

5. Ibid.

6. Unpublished address by Sandra K. Lackore, General Secretary and Treasurer, GCFA Annual Meeting (November 28, 2006), 1.

7. Jim Wallis, *God's Politics* (New York: HarperCollins, 2005), 22.

8. Paul Borden, *Hit the Bullseye* (Nashville: Abingdon Press, 2002), 125.

3. LEADERSHIP! LEADERSHIP! LEADERSHIP!

1. William H. Willimon, *Pastor: The Theology and Practice of Ordained Ministry* (Nashville: Abingdon Press, 1999), 34.

2. Obviously as a bishop of the church it should be understood that I am a clergyperson, coming to the office after more than thirty years as a pastor. I was licensed to preach in 1968, ordained a deacon in 1971, and an elder in 1974. By God's grace (and only that), I am still "going on toward perfection"—not there yet, just making the journey, following Jesus more closely each day. First, and above all, I am a baptized believer and Jesus-follower; then, having been called and credentialed, I am an ordained clergy; finally, I now serve in the office of bishop.

3. Robert E. Quinn, *Deep Change* (San Francisco: Jossey-Bass, 1996), 164.

4. Ibid., 165.

5. William H. Willimon, *Calling and Character* (Nashville: Abingdon Press, 2000), 22.

6. *The Works of John Wesley* (Grand Rapids, Mich.: Baker Books, 2002, reprinted from the 1872 edition), vol. 10, 481.

7. Ibid., 482.

8. Ibid.

9. Margaret J. Wheatley, *Leadership and the New Science* (San Francisco: Berrett-Koehler, 1992), 136.

10. Zander and Zander, *The Art of Possibility*, 162.

11. Paul D. Borden, *Direct Hit* (Nashville: Abingdon Press, 2006), 76.

12. Larry M. Goodpaster, "Exercising the Mind for Spiritual Leadership," *Circuit Rider* (January-February 2004): 10.

4. CORE COMPETENCIES FOR CHURCH LEADERSHIP

1. Dietrich Bonhoeffer, *The Cost of Discipleship* (New York: Touchstone, 1995), 89.

2. From the Charles Wesley hymn, "And Can It Be?" *The United Methodist Hymnal*, 1989, 363.

3. Thomas Merton, *The Inner Experience* (New York: HarperCollins, 2003), 92.

4. Carol Cartmill and Yvonne Gentile, *Leadership Essentials* (Nashville: Abingdon Press, 2006), 33.

5. *Wesley's 52 Standard Sermons* (Salem, Ohio: Schmul Publishing Co., 1988), 22.

6. Spelling consistent with *The Book of Discipline*.

7. Quinn, *Deep Change*, 34–35.

5. VITAL SIGNS OF DYNAMIC CONGREGATIONS

1. Philip Jenkins, *The Next Christendom* (New York: Oxford, 2002), 2.

2. Spencer Johnson, *Who Moved My Cheese?* (New York: G. P. Putnam's Sons, 1998).

3. N. T. Wright, *Simply Christian* (New York: HarperOne, 2006), 122.

4. Borden, *Direct Hit*, 76.

5. John Wesley, *52 Standard Sermons*, 401.

6. Margaret J. Wheatley and Myron Kellner-Rogers, *A Simpler Way* (San Francisco: Barrett-Koehler Publishers, 1996), 40–41.

7. Wright, *Simply Christian*, 200.

8. The ideas in this paragraph were shared with me by Walker Epps, district superintendent of the Marianna–Panama City District, Alabama–West Florida Conference. I am grateful for his insights and suggestions.

9. Wright, *Simply Christian*, 204.

10. *The Book of Discipline* (2004), The United Methodist Church, paragraph 120, 87.

6. GOING ON TO . . . GREATNESS

1. Jim Collins, *Good to Great* (New York: HarperCollins, 2002), 1.

2. Jim Collins, *Good to Great and the Social Sectors* (New York: Harper-Collins, 2005), 1.

3. Ibid., 31.

4. Collins, *Good to Great*, 208.

5. Kenneth J. Collins, *John Wesley: A Theological Journey* (Nashville: Abingdon Press, 2003), 263.

6. Richard P. Heitzenrater, *Wesley and the People Called Methodists* (Nashville: Abingdon Press, 1995), 3.

7. Ibid., 31.

8. Ibid., 130.

9. George G. Hunter III, *Christian Evangelical & . . . Democrat?* (Nashville: Abingdon Press, 2006), 50.

10. John Wesley, "Causes of the Inefficacy of Christianity," *The Works of John Wesley*, vol. 7 (Grand Rapids, Mich.: Baker Books, 2002), 282.

11. Ibid., 285.

12. Ibid., 286–87.

13. Hunter, *Christian Evangelical & . . . Democrat?*, 38, 40.

14. *Works of John Wesley*, Vol. 10, 496.

15. Collins, *John Wesley: A Theological Journey*, 194.

16. Wesley, *52 Standard Sermons*, 249.

17. Scott Jones, *Evangelistic Love of God and Neighbor* (Nashville: Abingdon Press, 2003), 114.

18. Brad J. Kallenberg, *Live to Tell* (Grand Rapids, Mich.: Brazos, 2002), 64.

19. Laceye C. Warner, "Offer Them Christ," in Paul Chilcote, *The Wesleyan Tradition* (Nashville: Abingdon Press, 2002), 164.

20. Kallenberg, *Live to Tell*, 37.

21. Jones, *Evangelistic Love of God and Neighbor*, 118.

22. Heitzenrater, *Wesley and the People Called Methodists*, 125.

23. Hunter, *Christian Evangelical & . . . Democrat?*, 4.

24. Keith H. Hammonds, "How Google Grows . . . and Grows . . . and Grows," *Fast Company* (April 2003): 74–81.

25. "Love Divine, All Loves Excelling," *The United Methodist Hymnal*, 384.

7. INNOVATION, FLEXIBILITY, AND THE CONNECTION

1. As the *Book of Resolutions* is specifically geared toward those statements and positions in keeping with the social principles of the denomination, it really is not surprising that no resolutions deal with membership loss or evangelism. The issue, however, is that we have neglected that Wesleyan evangelical spirit that must be the underpinning for all of our actions in and for the good of humanity.

2. Dominic Dodd and Ken Favaro, "Managing the Right Tension," *Harvard Business Review* (December, 2006): 73–74.

3. Chuck Salter, "Catering to the Masses," *Fast Company* (May, 2006): 55.

4. Ibid.

5. Collins, *Good to Great and the Social Sectors*, 14.

6. Salter, "Catering to the Masses," 56.

7. Zander and Zander, *The Art of Possibility*, 117.

8. Salter, "Catering to the Masses," 57.

9. Ibid., 57.

10. Stephen R. Covey, *The 8th Habit* (New York: Free Press, 2004), 69.

8. KEEPING HOPE ALIVE

1. Tom Peters, *Leadership* (New York: Dorling Kindersley Limited, 2005), 19.

2. Miroslav Volf, "Not Optimistic," *The Christian Century* (December 28, 2004): 31.

3. Zander and Zander, *The Art of Possibility*, 182.

4. Lencioni, *Silos, Politics and Turf Wars*, 107.

5. Ibid., 187.

6. Quinn, *Deep Change*, 198.

7. Although hallway conversations among several bishops have raised some of the concerns outlined here, this portion in no way reflects the thinking of the entire council. I do not question the loyalty, commitment, or motivation of any of us. I hope the leadership for transforming hope on behalf of The United Methodist Church begins within the council and moves ultimately to the whole church.

8. Quinn, *Deep Change*, 43.

9. Friedman, *The World Is Flat*, 201.

10. Albert C. Outler, *Evangelism and Theology in the Wesleyan Spirit* (Nashville: Discipleship Resources, 1996), 39.

11. Adam Hamilton, *Leading Beyond the Walls* (Nashville: Abingdon Press, 2002), 22.

12. Lencioni, *Silos, Politics and Turf Wars*, 206.